To Darling Th[illegible]

Thank you for a memorable evening at Central Criminal Court no 1!!

[illegible]

March 2009.

LEGAL HABITS

A Brief Sartorial History of Wig, Robe and Gown

LEGAL HABITS

A Brief Sartorial History of Wig, Robe and Gown

Thomas Woodcock

Ede and Ravenscroft

PRODUCED FOR EDE AND RAVENSCROFT LIMITED

BY GOOD BOOKS (GB PUBLICATIONS LTD)

50 QUEEN ANNE STREET, LONDON, W1M OHQ

ISBN 0 946555 56 7

EDITOR: DOMINIQUE ENRIGHT

DESIGN: DESIGN PRINCIPALS, WARMINSTER

ORIGINATION: COLOURWISE-KCO

PRINTED AND BOUND IN SINGAPORE BY TIEN WAH PRESS

ILLUSTRATION SOURCES

COLLEGE OF ARMS (PAGE) 62, 63; EDE & RAVENSCROFT 43, 48, 49, 50, 56, 57, 60, 66, 67, 68, 69, 70, 71; INNER TEMPLE 52, 53, 54; JANET GRANT 36; MARY EVANS PICTURE LIBRARY 10.

ALL OTHER ILLUSTRATIONS COURTESY OF THE AUTHOR.

Acknowledgements

Corporate grants of arms by the English Kings of Arms can be traced back to a grant to the Drapers' Company in 1439 and I was delighted to act for Ede and Ravenscroft in the grant to celebrate their Tercentenary in 1989. In the same year they produced their magnificently illustrated *Robes of the Realm* written by Una Campbell. This led Michael Middleton, the chairman of Ede and Ravenscroft, to ask me to do some research on wigs, and I should first like to thank him for his patience and enthusiasm without which this would never have appeared. I also owe a large debt to my research assistant Dr Nicholas de Somogyi, who did the initial work. Dominique Enright has been a most competent editor and to her I owe the suggestion of adding Judges' Robes to the initial work on Wigs and the Barrister's Gown. It is almost impossible to write anything on the subject of legal dress without copying the work of the foremost authority, Professor John Baker, and I am most grateful to him for looking at what I have written and correcting the worst mistakes. The Chapter of the College of Arms is to be thanked for permission to illustrate Sir Philip Sidney's Funeral Roll and I am particularly grateful to the Archivist Robert Yorke for many years of scholarly assistance. The staff of Ede and Ravenscroft, and in particular Christopher Allan, have been perpetually good-humoured and helpful and are to be thanked for a number of illustrations. Janet Grant must be thanked for endless typing of the text when trying to concentrate on medieval heraldry and also for supplying a picture of W. L. Mansel in an Episcopal wig. The original pictures in The Courts of Chancery, King's Bench, Exchequer and Common Pleas are the property of The Masters of the Bench of the Inner Temple. The Hon. Mr Justice Blackburne, who is responsible for the Costume Exhibition at the Royal Courts of Justice, and His Honour Judge Samuels are to be thanked for being photographed to illustrate judicial dress, and thanks are also due to Glenys Macdonald, Clerk to the Rt. Hon. Lord Justice May, and to Emma Pemberton, Deputy Private Secretary to The Lord Chief Justice, for their assistance. Finally, John Rogers is to be thanked for much of the photography.

FOREWORD

As Chairman of Ede and Ravenscroft I am delighted that Thomas Woodcock, Norroy and Ulster King of Arms, has written this book on wigs and gowns, maintaining the links which have existed for three centuries between the College of Arms and this firm. Since Thomas Ravenscroft founded his wig-making business in 1726 at 3 Serle Street, Lincoln's Inn, we have supplied wigs to the legal profession. The robe-making business of Joseph Webb Ede, who married Rosanna Ravenscroft in 1871, can be traced back to the seventeenth century, and robes and gowns have been worn by judges and barristers since medieval times. This account puts wigs in their historical context and shows how they were originally adopted as an item of fashion but retained by the Bar and Judiciary after they ceased to be fashionable. The wearing of wigs makes the administration of justice impersonal and with gowns contributes to uniformity of dress in court proceedings, which helps to emphasise the formal gravity and dignity of justice.

MICHAEL MIDDLETON
Chairman
Ede and Ravenscroft

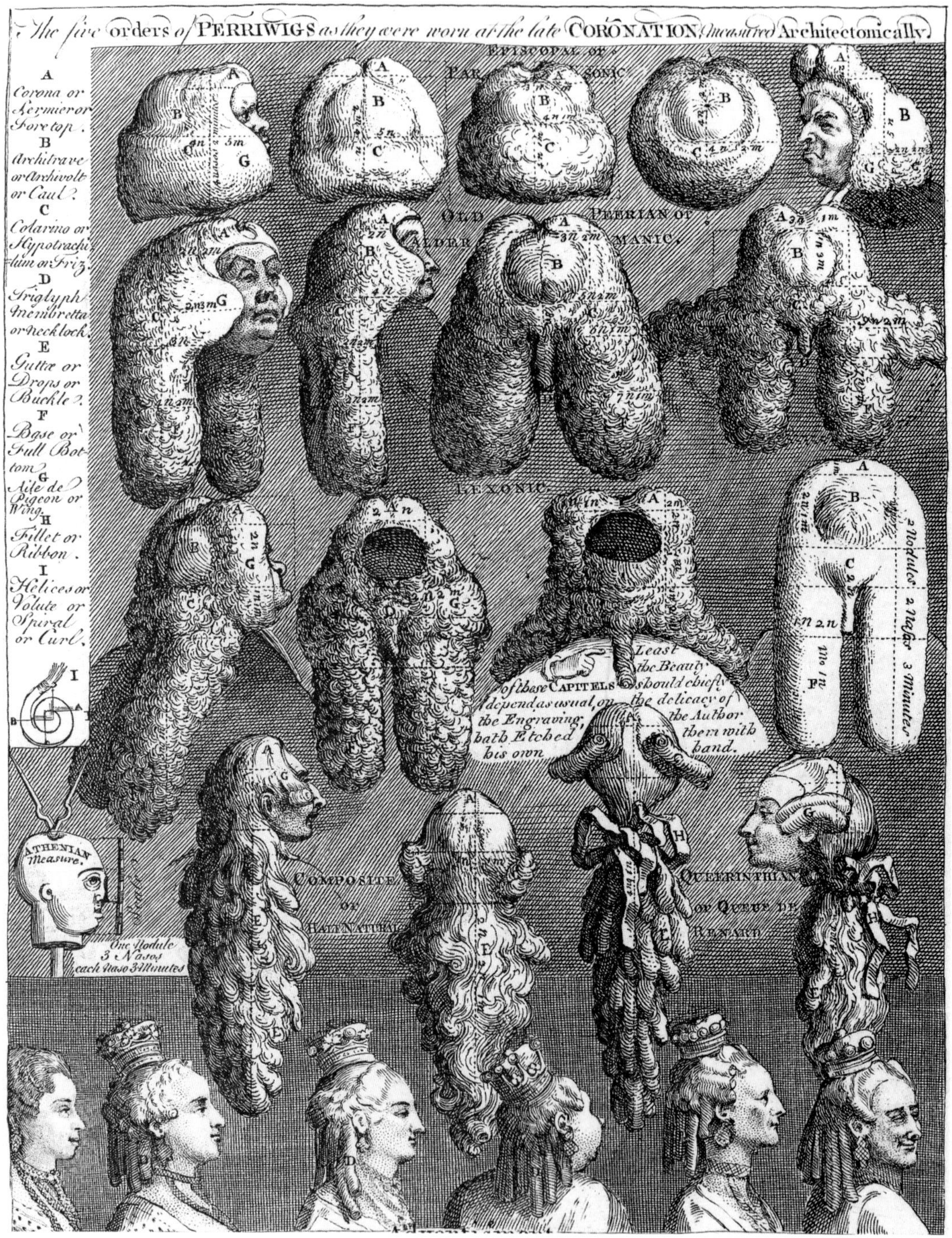

William Hogarth's The Five Orders of Periwigs as they were worn at the late Coronation measured Architectonically *(1761). Legal wigs, described as Lexonic, are in the third row after Episcopal or Parsonic in the first row and Old Peerian or Aldermanic in the second row. Hogarth calls an exaggerated fashionable wig in the fourth row 'Queerinthian'*

'Can Thus Large Wigs our Reverence Engage?'

. . . very handsome, and new periwig, make a great show.
SAMUEL PEPYS, DIARY, MARCH 1667

As suggested by this entry in Pepys's *Diary*, by the late 1660s wigs had become an important part of the fashionable person's wardrobe. It is from this general fashion that the use of wigs by the British legal profession stems, the difference in styles between those worn today by judges and those worn by barristers originating in the distinct fashions in wigs that developed during the course of the eighteenth century. Any account of legal wigs must therefore begin with a history of wigs as a general fashion.

The wearing of wigs originated long before they became fashionable in Europe, and it is known that from about 3000 BC wigs – made from real hair or sheep's wool – were a requirement among the well-dressed nobility of Ancient Egypt. Nearer to home, however, sources vary as to the exact dating of the introduction of wigs into the polite society of early modern Europe. The matter is obscured by the blurred distinction between wigs worn to disguise hair-loss and those deliberately adopted as a mark of fashion. (Ironically, hair-loss was itself sometimes the result of fashion, especially among women: the immediately recognisable sign of the aristocrat was a pale complexion – and the upper classes, to ensure this desirable paleness, used facial make-up based on white lead, which, as well as damaging the skin, caused hair to fall out.)

It is generally thought that Henry III of France (reigned 1574–89) inaugurated the vogue for false hair amongst his countrymen when he took to wearing headgear fringed with curls to disguise his premature baldness. Elizabeth I of England is also said to have worn a bright red wig in her later years to conceal her thinning grey hair (indeed, she is said to have owned more than eighty wigs). Women in fact seem to have incorporated artificial hair into their attire long before men and there is evidence to suggest that wigs formed part of a lady's fashionable dress in the sixteenth century. Robert Wilson's play *The Cobbler's Prophecy* (1594) satirises such trends: 'To day hir owne hair best becomes, which yellow is as gold,/A perriwigs better for to morrow, blacker to behold.'

Samuel Pepys (1633–1703) in a long Full-bottomed Wig. His Diary *records that he began to wear one on 3 November 1663. (After G. Kneller)*

A late-seventeenth-century annotation on a record of the 1574 Heralds' Visitation of Kent in the College of Arms, gives a 'translation', marking one of the stages in the word's Anglicisation, identifying the charges on the arms of Harman as '3 perukys vulgo Periwigs'. (When it was granted to Henry Harman, Clerk of the Crown, in 1498, the coat was described as a Chevron between three Scalps of Hair, perhaps a punning reference to his surname – Ha[i]rman – rather than to his occupation as Clerk of the Crown.)

It is from the French that the English word 'wig' derives, the French *perruque* undergoing a variety of Anglicisations and corruptions through the sixteenth and seventeenth centuries; these include 'perewincle' (1580; nothing to do with the flower periwinkle, whose name has a different derivation), 'perug' (1581), 'perwyke'(1588), 'perewincke' (1597) and the more usual 'perewig', 'perriwig' or, the most commonly seen, 'periwig' and 'peruke'. (The word is thought ultimately to derive from the Latin *pilus*, meaning a hair.)

In England wigs were at first associated either with vanity over hair-loss, newfangled female fashion, or with the histrionics of the stage, as part of the costume worn by actors. Shakespeare's Hamlet, for example, when warning the players against over-acting, declares, 'O, it offends me to the soul to hear a robustious periwig-pated fellow tear a passion to tatters, to very rags, to split the ears of the groundlings.' Hamlet's reference in part alludes to the practice of actors, inherited from Ancient Greek and Roman theatre, of wearing artificial hair and beards as part of their character. John Milton's Puritan pamphlet *Animadversions upon the Remonstrants Defence* (1641) associates wigs with the spurious arguments of his opponents and seeks to 'have the Periwiggs pluk't off that cover your baldness'.

In France, however, wigs were beginning to assume the aura of prestige. In 1620 the Abbé de la Rivière attended the court of Louis XIII at Versailles wearing a periwig simulating long fair hair, and within four years the King too had adopted the fashion. By 1634 there were forty barber-wigmakers at Louis XIII's court. His son Louis XIV (reigned 1643–1715), who favoured a voluminous black wig, created a guild of 200 barber-wigmakers in 1673.

English hairstyles in the first half of the century may account for the alacrity with which the periwig was subsequently adopted. Although the Puritan Parliamentarian faction were known as Roundheads from the short, sober cut of their hair, men's hair was being worn increasingly long from about 1610, reaching the shoulders by 1630. Even Cromwell, in common with the Interregnum fashion, wore his hair 'as long as it would grow'. By the time of the Restoration it had become fashionable to tie a ribbon into the shoulder-length hair.

After Charles I's execution in 1649 his son fled to France. It is from his return to England and his accession to the restored throne in 1660 that England's adoption of the French fashion may be dated. The wigs popularised from the French court by the King and his entourage imitated natural hair and were worn unpowdered. Men of fashion first began to shave their heads to wear wigs at this time, thus decisively marking

Charles II (1630–85) in a wig, a fashion he adopted from France in 1664. (Mezzotint portrait by A. Blooteling, 1680, after Lely)

the distinction between wigs worn as a cosmetic disguise and those displayed as a fashionable accessory.

Samuel Pepys (1633–1703) documents in his *Diary* the gradual adoption of the fashion. His entry for 9 May 1663 reveals his reluctance to part with his own hair: 'At Mr Jervas's, my old barber, I did try two or three borders and periwigs, meaning to wear one; and yet I have no stomach for it, but that the pains of keeping my hair clean is so great.' He here touches upon one practical reason for the popularity of wigs – hair could be cut very short which meant it was a great deal easier to keep clean and free of infestation from parasites, an important consideration at a time when there was no hot running water. Six months later, on 2 November 1663, Pepys records that he has heard 'the Duke [of York, Charles II's younger brother, the future James II] say he was going to wear a periwig; and they say the King also will'. Prompted perhaps by this rumour, he had his own head shaved the next day:

> I home, and by and by comes Chapman, the periwig-maker, and [upon] my liking it, without more ado I went up, and there he cut off my hair, which went a little to my heart at present to part with it; but, it being over, and my periwig on, I paid him £3 for it; and away went he with my own hair to make up another ... Went to Sir W. Pen ... [who] observed mightily, and discoursed much upon my cutting off my hair, as he do of everything that concerns me: but it is over, and so I perceive after a day or two it will be no great matter.

'No great matter' is made of his wig, he noted, at his office on the next day, and on 13 November he bought 'a second periwig, made of my own hair'. Within six months the trend had received its royal seal of approval. Pepys 'saw the King with his periwig, but not altered at all' at Hyde Park on 18 April 1664. An entry from a year later perhaps marks the transition from passing fad into enduring fashion: 'This day, after I had suffered my own hair to grow long in order to wearing it, I find the convenience of periwigs is so great, that I have cut off all short again, and will keep to periwigs' (5 May 1665).

These early wigs, like their French originals, aimed towards naturalism. They were parted in the centre, were flat on top and descended into a cascade of curls in blond, brown or black (the colour favoured by the King). They came to be known as Full-bottomed Wigs or Full-bottoms and their bulk and size grew greater and their appearance more artificial, as the seventeenth century wore on. In the 1680s these wigs began to follow women's more extravagant hairstyles (dressed high at the front, with curls on the forehead) and in the reign of James II (1685–8) achieved enormously cumbersome proportions, reaching waist-length by the 1690s. A woodcut from 1703 depicting a beau taking snuff, describes him as 'more Periwig than Man'.

As the fashion took hold in the later years of the seventeenth century, a variety of different styles and names of wig began to come into being, a trend which accelerated in the course of the eighteenth century, but is documented as early as 1688. Randle Holme ('Gentleman Sewer in extraordinary to his late Majesty King Charles 2. And sometimes Deputy for the Kings

117: 'A long Perawick with a pole lock'; 118: 'A Campaign or Travelling Wig' from Randle Holme, The Academy of Armory *(1688), p.452*

of Arms') included in his encyclopaedic *Academy of Armory, or Storehouse of Armory and Blazon,* a section on wigs that lists five 'Sorts of Perawicks' as follows.

◆ The first of these explains Pepys's 1663 reference to two or three borders and periwigs: '**A Border of Hair**,' writes Holme, 'is only Locks to cover the Ears and Neck, and is fixed to a Cap, having no head of hair.' This seems to have been the style worn by the French King Henry III a century before to disguise his baldness. A cross-reference in Holme's text refers back to an earlier section on hairdressing, which reads: 'Women usually wear such Borders which they call Curls or Locks when they hang over their ears.'

◆ '**A Short Bobb, a Head of Hair**, is a Wig that hath short Locks, and a hairy Crown.' The Bob Wig (as it came to be known) gathered up the unruly locks at the back of the Full-bottom and styled them into back-combed curls or bobs. It is thought that such wigs were first manufactured for those who could not afford a Full-bottom and it therefore came to be associated with tradesmen. In the eighteenth century, however, the Bob became a standard pattern among both the landed and professional classes. The so-called Long Bob covered the wearer's neck, while the Short Bob reached just below the ears.

◆ Holme's third style of wig is '**A Long Perawick** with **Side Hair** and a **Pole Lock** behind, which some term a Wig with a Sufflopin or with a Dildo'. This design is one of two illustrated in *The Academy of Armory* as appropriate to coats-of-arms. This '*long Curled Wig*' is drawn in rear view, and clearly shows the sausage-shaped corkscrew curl (or '*Sufflopin . . . Dildo* or *Pole-lock*') that formed a tail or queue at the nape of the neck between the wig's full-bottomed tresses. Holme's text describes it as follows:

> He beareth Argent, a *Peruque*, or *Perawick*, or a long *Perawick* with a *Pole Lock*, Sable. This is the Sign or Cognizance of the Perawick Maker. This is by Artists called a *long Curled Wig*, with a *Sufflopin*, or with a *Dildo* or *Pole-lock*.

While this twisted corkscrew curl or tail seems to have performed merely a decorative function, the impractical volume of the Full-bottom was elsewhere adapted for use by more active men, for example soldiers or travellers, as Holme's fourth example shows.

◆ This details '**A Campaign Wig**' as one that 'hath Knots or Bobs (or a Dildo on each side) with a Curled Forehead . . . also known as a *Travelling Wig*.' This style too is illustrated, viewed from the front and mounted on a wig-stand, and is described as follows:

> He beareth Sable, on a *Perawick Block*, fixed on a Stand, Or, a *Peruque* (or a *Campaign Wig*) with a Curled Foretop, and *Bobs*, Argent. This is a kind of *Travelling Wig*, having the side or bottom locks turned up into *Bobs* or *Knots*, tied up with Ribbons.

Instead of the single corkscrew tail or 'dildo' of the Full-bottom, the Campaign Wig gathered together the hair at the back and side of the wig into two great twists, tapered into two knotted tails, for a more manageable style.

◆ The '**Grafted Wig**' is the fifth of Holme's examples, though the exact status of this 'Perawick with a turn on the top of the head, in imitation of a Mans hairy Crown' is unclear. Perhaps it anticipates the later style, introduced in the 1730s, known as the Toupet, Top or Foretop, in which, instead of dressing a wig with a central parting, its hair was brushed straight up at the front and mingled with the wearer's own hair at the forehead beneath it.

A French print of Hans William Bentinck (1649–1709), 1st Earl of Portland, KG, in a Full-bottomed Wig when Ambassador to France in 1698

These 'Sorts of Perawicks' continued to subdivide long into the eighteenth century, and the refinements Holme documents (the Short Bob, the Pole-Lock, the Travelling or Campaign Wig) foreshadow the trend for smaller wigs that was to become dominant in the eighteenth century.

The Full-bottom 'reached its maximum grandeur' during the reign of Queen Anne (1702–14), but the range of smaller, more manageable wigs, available in a variety of names and styles, also took hold in this period and broadly characterises the wig's development in Georgian England, where particular styles increasingly indicated the age, place of residence, standing and even the profession of the wearer. The craze for these various styles of wig in the early 1700s was a repeated subject of the new coffee-house journalism.

In 1711, Joseph Addison (1672–1719), the essayist, poet and statesman, whose father was the Dean of Lichfield, claimed in an article in *The Spectator* that 'Great Masters in Painting never care for drawing People in the Fashion, as very well knowing that the Head-Dress, or Periwig, that now prevails, and gives a Grace to their Portraitures at present, will make a very odd Figure, and perhaps look monstrous, in the Eyes of Posterity.' Such a wig certainly 'gives a Grace' to Sir Godfrey Kneller's portrait of Sir Christopher Wren in the National Portrait Gallery, which was painted in that same year, 1711. (The last stone of St Paul's Cathedral was laid in 1710.) It shows the architect in a luxuriant natural-coloured Full-bottom reaching halfway down his back. Despite the 'very odd Figure' it perhaps presents today, an article in *The Spectator* from the following August, by Eustace Budgell (1686–1737), the son of Joseph Addison's first cousin, comments on the increased attention bestowed on the wearer by this type of wig: 'I have indeed my self observed, that my Banker ever bows lowest to me when I wear my full-bottom'd Wig; and writes me Mr. or Esq, accordingly as he sees me dress'd'; on the other hand, Budgell censures a 'very meanly dress'd' gentleman in a 'short Wig ... answerable to the rest of his apparel' for 'appearing in a Dress so much beneath his Quality and Estate'. An engraving of Budgell's own contemporary portrait, vividly shows him in a wig that rivals Wren's in size and prestige. The fashion for such styles of wig, however, was on the wane.

Addison's article proceeds to testify to the proliferation of new styles of wig in the period and contrasts the now old-fashioned styles worn in the country (which he likens to 'a Gallery of old Family-Pictures') with those at the 'height of the Mode' in London. This 'Variety of Garbs and Habits' is elaborated in the form of a letter from a gentleman lawyer of the Middle Temple, travelling on the Western Circuit. After encountering the 'greatest Beau at our next County Sessions . . . dressed in a most monstrous Flaxen Periwig, that was made in King *William*'s Reign', the writer meets 'a young Fellow riding towards us at full Gallop, with a Bob Wig and a black Silken Bag tied to it'.

Old and new styles are here brought into abrupt contrast. While the provincial beau's 'Flaxen Periwig' apparently describes a naturalistic, blond Full-bottom of the style popular in the reign of William III after the death of his wife Queen Mary in 1694 (till his own death in 1702), the young fellow's 'Bob Wig and ... black Silken Bag' is an early reference to another distinctive design of the eighteenth century known as the Bag Wig. The tail (or 'queue') of this style of wig was enclosed in a bag made of black satin or silk, variously known as a bag, purse, bourse (the French for 'purse') and crapaud (the French for 'toad', so named for the bag's squat, crouching shape). The open end of this bag enclosed the wig's tail and was secured by a drawstring, itself concealed within a broad, stiff, black decorative bow. Much as a Windsor-knot in the twentieth century referred to a particular style of tying a tie, one version of the Bag Wig was later known as the Rose-Bag by the particular styling of its knot.

The tone of Addison's description suggests there was something foppish about the Bag Wig and its associations in particular with French fashion continued throughout the eighteenth century. This is shown by a satirical poem of 1750 by Christopher Smart (1722–71) in the form of a dialogue between 'The Bag-wig and the Tobacco-Pipe':

> A Bag-wig of a jauntee air,
> Trick'd up with all a barber's care,
> Loaded with powder and perfume,
> Hung in a spendthrift's dressing-room;
> Close by its side, by chance convey'd,
> A black Tobacco-Pipe was laid.

When the wig complains of his 'fetid breath', the 'English pipe/Deem'd worthy of each Briton's gripe' calls him a 'flaunting French, fantastic bragger':

> 'Twas better for the English Nation
> Before such scoundrels came in fashion,
> When none sought hair in realms unknown,
> When every blockhead bore his own.

As the poem indicates, powder and perfume were an established part of the 'barber's care' by 1750. Wigs were generally worn naturally coloured (like the 'Flaxen Periwig ... made in King William's Reign' that Addison described in 1711) until around the beginning of the

William III (1650–1702) in Roman dress wearing a long Full-bottomed Wig. (Mezzotint by John Smith after W. Wissing & J. Vandervaart)

The Grand Procession from the Drawing Room to the Chapel Royal, St James's, on the marriage of the Prince of Wales *(Haines & Son, 1795). The Duke of Clarence, later William IV (1765–1837), in a Bag Wig with four tiers of buckles, leads the bride. The Gentleman Usher and two Heralds wear long Bob Wigs with bags*

eighteenth century, when scented hair powder came into general use to give hair or wigs a fashionably bleached look. One commentator from 1697 described the pioneers of this fashion as 'creatures compounded of a periwig; and a coat laden with powder as white as a miller's'. Wigs would be greased by barber-hairdressers on the heads of their clients and their faces then covered by a funnel-shaped bag while clouds of powder were blown onto their heads with a pair of bellows. The powder was usually white, but, later, grey, flaxen, brown and even blue varieties were sometimes adopted, which lent the wigs a range of artificial colour equivalent to the natural range of hair colour used in earlier Full-bottoms.

The proprietor of the German Shaving Machine wears a Tie Wig, his apprentice in the foreground dresses a wig traditionally whilst another employee discharges a hair-powdering gun along a line of wigs

By the time the lawyer in Joseph Addison's 1711 *Spectator* article reaches Cornwall, 'We fancied ourselves in King Charles the Second's Reign, the People having made very little Variations in their Dress since that time':

> We were indeed very much surprized, at the Place we lay at last Night, to meet a Gentleman that had accoutered himself in a Night-Cap Wig, a Coat with long Pockets and slit Sleeves with high Scollop Tops; but we soon found by his Conversation that he was a Person who laughed at the Ignorance and Rusticity of the Country People, and was resolved to live and die in the Mode.

The Nightcap Wig is another example of the smaller,

A Porcupine Wig. Like the Rough Scratch and Brutus Wigs for men, which resembled the wearer's own hair dishevelled, it exposed wig wearing to ridicule

more stylised models of wig that came into fashion in this period. In contrast to the voluminous Full-bottom of 'King Charles the Second's Reign', the Nightcap Wig was a close-fitting hairpiece with a short tail and small round head, named for its resemblance to a nightcap. In an article in *The Tatler* in 1709 Richard Steele (1672–1729), the essayist, dramatist and politician who was knighted in 1715 and whose father was a successful Dublin attorney, includes 'nightcap wigs' among the fashions worn by 'persons that dress themselves as they please, without regard to decorum'.

Addison satirises the bewildering changeability and variety of new fashions of wig: 'If instead of running after the Mode they would continue fix'd in one certain Habit,' he comments, 'the Mode would some time or other overtake them, as a Clock that stands still is sure to point right once in twelve Hours.' Another of Eustace Budgell's *Spectator* articles, in the following year, documents a further development of the trend. A comic letter purporting to be from a fashionable lady about town, 'Dorinda', claims that men are as subject to vanity as women, since 'The different Forms of their Wiggs, together with the various Cocks of their hats, all flatter us in this Opinion'. Dorinda could not, she says, recognise her suitor for his almost daily alteration in the fashion:

> I had an Humble Servant last summer, who the first time he declared himself, was in a Full-Bottom Wigg; but the Day after, to my no small surprize, he

> accosted me in a thin natural one. I receiv'd him, at this our Second Interview, as a perfect Stranger, but was extreamly confounded, when his Speech discovered who he was. I resolved, therefore, to fix his Face in my Memory for the future; but as I was walking in the Park the same Evening, he appeared to me in one of those Wiggs that I think you call a Night-cap, which had alter'd him more effectually than before. He afterwards played a couple of Black Riding-Wiggs upon me, with the same Success; and, in short, assumed a new face almost every Day in the First Month of his Courtship.

Though doubtless exaggerated, Budgell's portrayal of four different wigs in almost as many days – the Full-bottom, the 'thin natural one', the Nightcap and the Riding Wig (a form of stylised black Full-bottom apparently favoured by Richard Steele, Addison's friend and contemporary at Oxford) – marks the emergence of a sort of grammar of wigs, in much the same way that morning and evening dress came to be distinguished in the same period.

To Addison a style of wig was an index of fashion; to Budgell it revealed the wealth and standing of a 'Man of Mode'. To the poet and dramatist, John Gay (1685–1732) the style of a man's wig comprised 'a kind of Index of the Mind'. Gay's essay in *The Guardian* from 1713 observed that just as 'Dress is grown of universal Use in the Conduct of Life', so the 'Sciences of Poetry and Dress have so near an Alliance to each other, that the Rules of the one, with very little variation, may serve for the other.' He associated varied fashions with different professions and qualities of mind:

> Others who lay the stress of Beauty in their Face, exert all their Extravagance in the Perriwig, which is a kind of Index of the Mind; the Full bottom formally combed all before, denotes the Lawyer and the Politician; the smart tie Wig with the black Ribbon shows a Man of fierceness of Temper; and he that burthens himself with a superfluity of white Hair which flows down the Back, and mantles in waving Curles over the Shoulders, is generally observed to be less curious in the furniture of the inward recesses of the Skull.

The 'formally combed' Full-bottomed Wig acts as a sort of frame for the oratory issuing from the mouth of the lawyer or politician. By contrast, the 'superfluity of white Hair', with its long curls, evidently describes a more old-fashioned style of Full-bottom, and sustains the satire of 'the Beau's character' in Thomas Baker's 1706 comedy *Hampstead Heath*, which pithily rhymes 'A wig that's full' with 'An empty skull'. The third of

Gay's styles, 'the smart tie Wig with the black Ribbon', is an early reference to another major eighteenth-century trend.

While the Bob Wig back-combed the locks of the Full-bottom into a shoulder-length or neck-length ridge of more manageable bobs or curls (the Long Bob and Short Bob, respectively); and while the Bag Wig tightly drew back the wig's tail into a decorative bag or crapaud; the Tyed, Tye or Tie Wig styled the wig's back-hair into a single bunch tied at the nape of the neck by a black ribbon bow. It shows, in Gay's words, 'a Man of fierceness of Temper' because the style was originally associated with the military profession. George Farquhar (1678–1707) in *The Recruiting Officer* (published 1706) includes among the attributes of a captain, 'a fierce knot in my periwig'.

The Ramillies Wig, a variant of the Tie Wig, was named after the Duke of Marlborough's victory against the French at the Battle of Ramillies in 1706. Its style resembled that of the Campaign Wig described by Randle Holme in 1688 but instead of the tresses of the Full-bottom being twisted into two 'Bobs or Knots, tied up with Ribbons', in the Ramillies Wig the hair was gathered at the back into a single, tapering, thickly-plaited tail that was tied with two bows, one at the nape of the neck, and a smaller one, at the tip of the queue, which hung down to the small of the wearer's back. The tail of later models of Tie Wig (the Short Queue, for example, or the Physical Tie) was shorter, extending to just beyond the wearer's collar.

An engraving by William Hogarth (1697–1764), dating from around 1725, apparently confirms Gay's assertion in 1713 that 'the Full bottom formally combed all before, denotes the Lawyer'. Entitled *The Triple Plea*, the print shows how the representatives of 'Law, Physick, and Divinity / Contend which shall Superior be'. From left to right: a gowned lawyer holds a legal document; a clergyman, with a prayer-book in one hand, points towards heaven with the other; and a doctor holds up a bottle of medicine – yet each, as the text puts it, is silent 'Without a Fee'. This 'early assault on the growth and institutionalisation of the professions', in the words of David Bindman, author of *Hogarth and his Times,* is careful to distinguish between the styles of the three men's wigs. The lawyer, pictured in right profile, is wearing a Full-bottom reaching down to his chest, and a small queue can be seen at the nape of his neck. The wig closely resembles Holme's 'long Curled Wig, with a Sufflopin'. The clergyman, seen from the front, is wearing a Long Bob, parted in the middle of the forehead, covering the

Louis XVIII (1755–1824) in 1814, the year of his first Restoration to the throne of France, wearing a Tie Wig with pigeon's wings, giving him an old-fashioned appearance. (J. C. Stadler after C. Rosenberg)

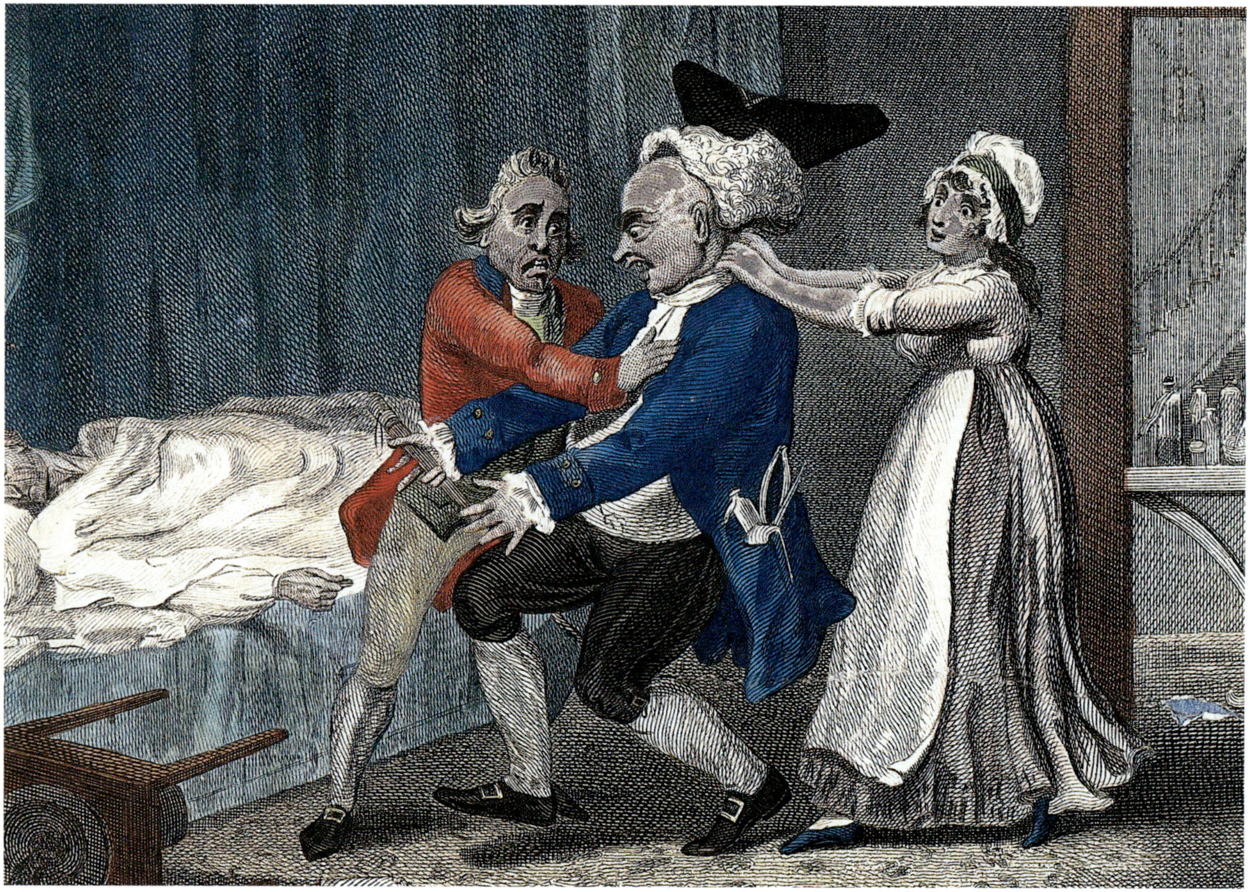

The Doctor snatching at the guinea after his patient is dead *illustrates the Physical Wig, a form of Bob Wig worn by doctors*

back of his neck. The physician, seen in left profile, is wearing a form of Tie Wig in which the lower tresses of hair are tied into three bunches of loose curls which were known as 'pigeon's wings'. The two ties in the side-lock hanging over the left shoulder are clearly visible.

Hogarth's print illustrates the eighteenth-century trend, indicated by Gay, for particular styles of wig to denote distinct professions. A number of wigs came to be called after the profession of their wearers. For example the Lion Wig – a Long Bob named for its resemblance to a lion's mane – was also called the Physical Wig since it was worn by members of the medical profession. The minor poet William Woty (?1731–91) includes a description of such a wig in his poem 'The Caxon'*(1760), which is devoted to the theme of wigs:

> What! shall my spirits droop, because my Pate
> With all the pomp that bushy Hair can boast
> Is not surrounded! such as busy child
> Of lordly Physick oft presumes to wear,
> Index of knowledge and of thought profound!

With Christopher Smart, Woty also notes that it is the 'dress-enraptur'd beau,/ Fashion's Apprentice, Affectation's Child' who 'In Bag-Wigg glory struts', and the same sense of an accepted propriety, by which certain professions wore certain wigs, illuminates James Boswell's later comment to Dr Johnson, which he recorded in his *Life of Johnson*, that 'There is a general levity in the age. We have physicians now with bag-wigs' (15 April 1778). The Bishop's, Episcopal or Parsonic Wig, a style of Short Bob, is another example of this eighteenth-century dress code, while military men retained the Ramillies Wig long after the battle that gave it its name.

Sir Walter Scott's novel *The Antiquary* (1816) describes the three wigs of its characters in an ascending order of volume, 'like the three degrees of comparison – Sir Arthur's Ramillies being the positive, his own bob-wig the comparative, and the overwhelming grizzle of the worthy clergyman figuring as the superlative'.

The Grizzle Wig, which Scott also calls 'the buzz wig', is first recorded by the *Oxford English Dictionary* in 1755. This was a style of grey or grizzled Full-bottom suitable for the older man, as a poem by Thomas Warton the Younger (1728–90), appointed Poet Laureate in 1785, demonstrates. The narrator of his 'Ode to a Grizzle Wig, by a Gentleman who had just left off his Bob' regrets the passing of his youth, embodied in the symbol of his new style of wig. 'At skittles, in a Grizzle, can I play?' he asks, commenting on the dignity it was thought to confer:

**Caxon was the name given to any wig that had lost its form and design through neglect and exposure to all weathers. Originally a' Caxton', it took its name from the Cambridgeshire village of Caxton near to which a murderer who had disguised himself in a wig was hanged.*

All hail, ye curls, that, rang'd in reverend row,
With snowy pomp my conscious shoulders hide!
That fall beneath in venerable flow,
And crown my brows above with feathery pride!
Can thus large Wigs our reverence engage?
Have Barbers thus the pow'r to blind our eyes?
Is science thus conferr'd on every sage,
By Bayliss, Blenkinsop, and lofty Wise?
But thou, farewell, my Bob! whose thin-wove thatch
Was stor'd with quips and cranks, and wanton wiles,
That love to live within the one-curl'd Scratch
With fun, and all the family of smiles.

Bayliss, Blenkinsop and Wise were three prominent Oxford wigmakers. The 'one-curl'd Scratch' referred to was a style of Short Bob that covered the back of the wearer's head and mingled at the forehead with his own hair. In the later eighteenth century the name was applied to a short, natural-looking wig designed to resemble the wearer's own hair. The Smooth Scratch was tidily dressed, while the Rough Scratch was styled to appear fashionably dishevelled.

As Warton's poem suggests, particular styles of wig, while designating the wearer's professional or social standing, were also an indicator of his age. This is illustrated by one of the 'Odd Advertisements from the

Wigs, *by M. Darby, October 1773. Left to right* (top row)*: a Short Bob with single tier of buckles, a Grizzle Wig, a Tie Wig with pigeon's wings, a*

Staring Wig and an Episcopal Wig; (second row) *a Bag Wig, a short Full-bottomed, a long Full-bottomed and a Campaign Wig*

Public Advertiser' reprinted in the *Annual Register* of 1759. The writer, whose initials are given as S.U. (perhaps a reference to Sylvanus Urban, the invented name, continued into the nineteenth century, for the editor of *The Gentleman's Magazine,* started in 1731 by the printer Edward Cave, 1691–1754) responds to a previous 'advertisement of a lady whose sentiments jump so entirely with mine, I am convinced we are cut out for each other':

> My person is far from disagreeable, my skin smooth and shining, my forehead high and polished; my eyes sharp, tho' small, my nose long and aquiline, my mouth wide and what teeth I have perfectly sound: all this, with the addition of a flaxen full bottom, suitable to the age of between forty and fifty, with a good heart and sweet disposition.

Warton's distinction between a youthful 'humble Bob' and the 'awe-diffusing hair' of a Full-bottom like S.U.'s, 'suitable to the age of between forty and fifty', anticipates the difference in style between the wigs worn today by judges and barristers.

The next significant advance in wig styles took place in the latter half of the eighteenth century. The side locks of the Tie, Bob or Bag Wigs were primped

H. Bunbury's The Siege of Namur by Capt Shandy & Corporal Trim. *Uncle Toby wears an outdated Ramillies Wig with a long plait*

out into voluminous bunches of loose curls known as 'pigeon's wings' (as worn by Hogarth's physician). While some types of wig continued to use this bunching effect (the expressively named Cauliflower Wig, for example), others replaced it by dressing the locks into cylindrical rolls, worn in horizontal rows or tiers, arranged about the side and back of the head, which were known as 'pipes' or 'buckles', from the French *boucle* meaning a curl.

Laurence Sterne's novel *The Life and Opinions of Tristram Shandy* (1759–67) testifies to the advent of this new style of buckled wig. In the ninth volume the

The Disappointed Nabob *(Sir Francis Sykes, MP), published in* The Town and Country Magazine, *1776. The buckles on the modern barrister's wig derive from this style*

Lord Le D– *(Sir Francis Dashwood, Lord Le Despencer), published in* The Town and Country Magazine, *1774. His wig has a single row of buckles*

narrator's Uncle Toby, an old soldier wounded at the Siege of Namur in 1692, prepares to go courting:

> Though the corporal [his servant Trim] had been as good as his word in putting my uncle Toby's great ramallie-wig into pipes, yet the time was too short to produce any great effects from it: it had lain many years squeezed up in the corner of his old campaign trunk . . . it curled everywhere but where the corporal would have it; and where a buckle or two, in his opinion, would have done it honour, he could as soon have raised the dead.

Though the timescale of Sterne's novel is complicated, the passage records an old man struggling to keep up with a new fashion. Caricatures in the *Town and Country Magazine* of the early 1770s illustrate the development of buckles. Sir Francis Dashwood, Bt (1708–81), Lord Le Despencer, wears, in 1774, a Bag Wig with a single tier of buckles. In 1776, the 'Disappointed Nabob', Sir Francis Sykes (1732–1804), 1st Bt of Basildon Park, wears a Bag Wig with two tiers of buckles. The modern barrister's wig derives from this style.

'In England,' commented Dr Johnson in 1778, 'any man who wears a sword and a powdered wig is ashamed to be illiterate.' Johnson died in 1784; the fashion for wigs did not long outlive him.

Bless me Ladies Is this I or My Brother. *Mezzotint published by H. Bryer, typical of the many prints ridiculing Staring Wigs worn by Macaroni 1764–72*

As with all fashion trends, styles of wig-coiffure tended, during the 150 years of their vogue, to oscillate between extremes. Just as Full-bottoms had ballooned to waist-length at the end of the seventeenth century, only to be superseded by shorter, more stylised wigs in the 1710s; so in the mid-1760s, as the trimmer buckle-style of wig became standard, a group of young men took to wearing exaggeratedly large wigs, called Staring

Now Sr You'r a Compleat Macaroni, *printed and sold for C. McLean, Edinburgh. Note the huge folded knot of hair worn behind a Staring Wig*

Wigs, together with tightly fitting, multi-coloured clothes and spying glasses. They became known as Macaroni after the club they formed in London in 1764 devoted to Italianate designs of food and fashion, which lasted till 1772. The powdered wigs they wore accentuated the effect of the Toupet Wigs of the 1730s, and were brushed up from the forehead into a single great peak, with an immense folded knot of hair worn behind. Within a generation, however, the fashion had once again reversed, this time terminally.

On 30 April 1795 'An Act for granting to His Majesty [George III] a Duty on Certificates issued for using Hair Powder' was published effective from 5 May. This levied a tax of one guinea a year on hair powdering and was said to have raised £20,000 in the first year despite the advance opposition reported in *The Times* of 14 April 1795:

> A numerous club has been formed in Lambeth, called the Crop Club, every member of which, on his entrance, is obliged to have his head docked as close as the Duke of Bridgewater's old-bay coach-horses. This assemblage is instituted for the purpose of opposing, or rather evading the tax on powdered heads.

Prompted by this taxation and perhaps influenced by the

more austere spirit of the French Revolution, the general fashion for wigs in England at last began to wane. In contrast to the exaggerated style of the Macaroni, it became fashionable once more to wear one's own hair in a close-cut style. One such hairstyle was known as the Brutus, after the idealist Roman republican, but though such a thing as a Brutus Wig – a style of unpowdered, natural-brown and dishevelled Scratch Wig – was available in England in the first decade of the nineteenth century, 'the convenience of periwigs' that Pepys had commended in 1665 lost the battle to natural hair.

'The Caxon', William Woty's 1760 paean to the robust, multi-purpose wig-style of that name, details the burdensome rituals of the 'nicest care' of 'oil or powder . . . pendent on a peg, or soft reclin'd/Within the concave of inclosing Box,/Else all their fine œconomy is lost' that the maintenance of eighteenth-century wigs required. The preface by Richard Fenton (1746–1821) of his *Memoirs of an Old Wig* (1815) acknowledges the passing of the vogue:

> The prevailing fashion affects to imitate the natural hair, as it is now worn, without powder, and combed negligently; and when the present generation of men turned fifty, shall have passed away, the rising one, from the disuse of powder, hot irons, and other artifices, destructive of the hair, by soon turning it grey, or producing premature baldness, is not likely to adopt the Wig, so that soon the use of it bids fair to be confined to the three learned professions of Divinity, Law and Physic.

As the Classical era yielded to the Romantic, Fenton's suspicion that the generation subsequent to 'men turned fifty' in 1815 were abandoning the wig proved true as European fashion moved on: while, for example, Mozart (1756–91) and Dr Johnson (1709–84) both wore a wig, neither Beethoven (1770–1827), nor Wordsworth (1770–1850) ever did. In September 1798, Samuel Taylor Coleridge (1772–1834) met Friedrich Klopstock (1724–1803), author of the biblical epic *Der Messias*, whom he called 'the venerable father of German poetry'. He described their encounter in a letter home, clearly taken aback by the great powdered wig Klopstock was wearing, a 'Trick & Fashion' against Nature which he thought was as ridiculous as topiary: '. . . as when you see Yews clipped into miserable peacocks. The author of the *Messiah* should have worn his own Grey Hair.'

In England, perhaps because of the prestige and authority they had denoted, wigs continued to be worn by Fenton's 'three learned professions' well into the

Portrait sketches of Voltaire (1694–1778) in a variety of wigs, principally short Full-bottomed

nineteenth century, however; and, in the case of the law, into the twenty-first. Among doctors, soldiers and clergymen they were only relinquished by slow degrees.

Maria Edgeworth's 1814 novel *Patronage* includes a scene illustrating the resistance to change among the older generation. The elderly Mr Panton berates a young physician for not wearing a wig:

> 'Why, Sir, in my youth every decent physician wore a wig and I have no notion of a good physician without a wig – particularly a young one. – Sir, many people have a great objection to a young physician for many reasons. – And take my advice in time, Doctor Percy – a wig, a proper wig, not one of your modern natural scratches, but a decent powdered Doctor's bob.'

Percy replies that, as far as he can see, his patients 'would feel it a matter of indifference whether they were restored to health by a Doctor in a wig, or without one'.

Resistance was felt among military men too. In the second half of the eighteenth century, army officers, in common with other gentlemen, wore powdered wigs, but as wigs became increasingly impractical on the battlefield, only the senior officers retained the fashion. In the preface to his *Memoirs of an Old Wig*, for example, Fenton records that 'General Whitford, Colonel of the 19th Regiment, was known throughout the army, by the name of White Wig. The two Generals Pattison were also designated by the titles of Queue and Toupee.' Further down the ranks soldiers plaited and greased their own hair into queues or pigtails (resembling the single queue of the earlier Ramillies Wig), which were combined with hair-extensions and stiffened with pipe-clay. The length of these regimental queues was specified to be nine inches (fourteen among the Guards). An illustration of *Camp Scenes* by W. H. Pyne (1769–1843) from 1803 depicts two soldiers having their queues dressed.

The use of hair powder was abolished in the British army in the 1790s and the dressed queue was discontinued by general order on 20 July 1808:

> . . . in consequence of the state of preparation for immediate service in which the whole army is at present moment to be held, His Majesty has been graciously pleased to dispense with the use of queues until further orders.

Hair was to be 'cut close in their necks in the neatest and most uniform manner', and frequently washed, for which purpose a sponge was to 'be added to each man's regimental necessaries'. The queues cut from the heads

George IV (1762–1830), the first British Sovereign since Charles II to wear his own hair

of men of the 28th Regiment were collected on board their headquarters ship and 'by a signal, the whole were hove overboard, with three cheers'. Lieutenant-Colonel Donnellan of the 48th Regiment of Foot, however, was nicknamed 'the last of the powderers' since he ignored both these directives and continued to wear a long, powdered queue until 1809 when he was killed at the Battle of Talavera.

The fashion for wigs was slow to disappear entirely from the heads of the clergy too. Despite some initial opposition, clergymen had adopted the fashion for wigs as part of their canonical attire by the time of the Glorious Revolution (1688) and by the end of the eighteenth century, as the 'Parson's feathertop, frizzed broad and high' – referred to by George Colman the elder (1732–94) in the Prologue to *Bon Ton* (1775) – the Bishop's, Episcopal or Parsonic wig and Sir Walter Scott's 'overwhelming grizzle of the worthy clergyman' demonstrate, the fashion was inseparable from this profession as well. 'Wigs were worn by Bishops in the House of Lords until 1830, when Charles James Blomfield (1786–1857), Bishop of London, obtained the permission of William IV for the Episcopal bench to discontinue the practice,' J. Stevens Cox tells us in *An Illustrated Dictionary of Hairdressing and Wigmaking*. As late as 1858, John Bird Sumner (1780–1862), Archbishop of Canterbury from 1848, presided over the marriage of the Princess Royal and Frederick III of Germany wearing a wig.

A century before, in 1760, William Woty had predicted that

> The Bob shall fade away, the Major's Lock
> Shall drop its Curl, and Scratches shrink in wear
> But thou, my Caxon, thou shalt be the same.

W. L. Mansel (1753–1820), Bishop of Bristol (1808–20), in an Episcopal Wig. (Hand-tinted etching by Dighton, 1810)

(The Major's Lock was a two-tailed military style of the Tie Wig.)

The general fashion for wigs did wane, except among lawyers, with whom the habit endures to this day.

◆◆◆

Apart from coachmen of the royal household the wig remains the prerogative solely of the British legal profession. Legal wigs began by imitating the general fashion and only later represented the profession of law. It is from the beginning of the eighteenth century, with the two defined styles of Full-bottomed and Tie Wig, that the modern distinction between a judge's dress wig and Bench wig (and barrister's court wig) originates.

When wigs first became fashionable in England the only connotations they bore were those of wealth and prestige, and barristers took to the vogue accordingly. Judges, however, 'at first thought them so "coxcombical" that they would not allow young members of the Bar to plead before them so attired'. Addison's letter in *The Spectator* of 28 July 1711 purports to have come from 'a Lawyer of the *Middle Temple*, a *Cornishman* by birth', and it is on the Western Circuit of the court system that he is able to observe the variety of newly modish styles, from the Nightcap to the Bag Wig, among members of the legal profession. By and large, however, barristers seem to have worn the longer, more old-fashioned styles when pleading in court in the period – or so a later *Spectator* article, in June 1712, again by Addison, implies. In it he contrasts a customary English reserve to the vivid, rhetorical gestures shown in '*Raphael*'s portrait of St. *Paul* preaching at Athens' and the 'Vehemence of Action' reported of Cicero and Demosthenes:

> How cold and dead a Figure in Comparison of these Great Men, does an Orator often make at the British Bar, holding up his Head with the most insipid Serenity and stroaking the sides of a long Wigg that reaches down to his Middle?

The words seem to confirm both Gay's appraisal from 1713 that the 'Full bottom formally combed all before denotes the Lawyer', and Hogarth's engraving of the Lawyer in a formally combed Full-bottom in *The Triple Plea*.

As time passed and barristers like these were promoted to the bench, they retained the fashions of their youth and continued to wear the Full-bottom style of wig, even as the general fashion for slighter, more manageable styles of Tie Wig came to be adopted by

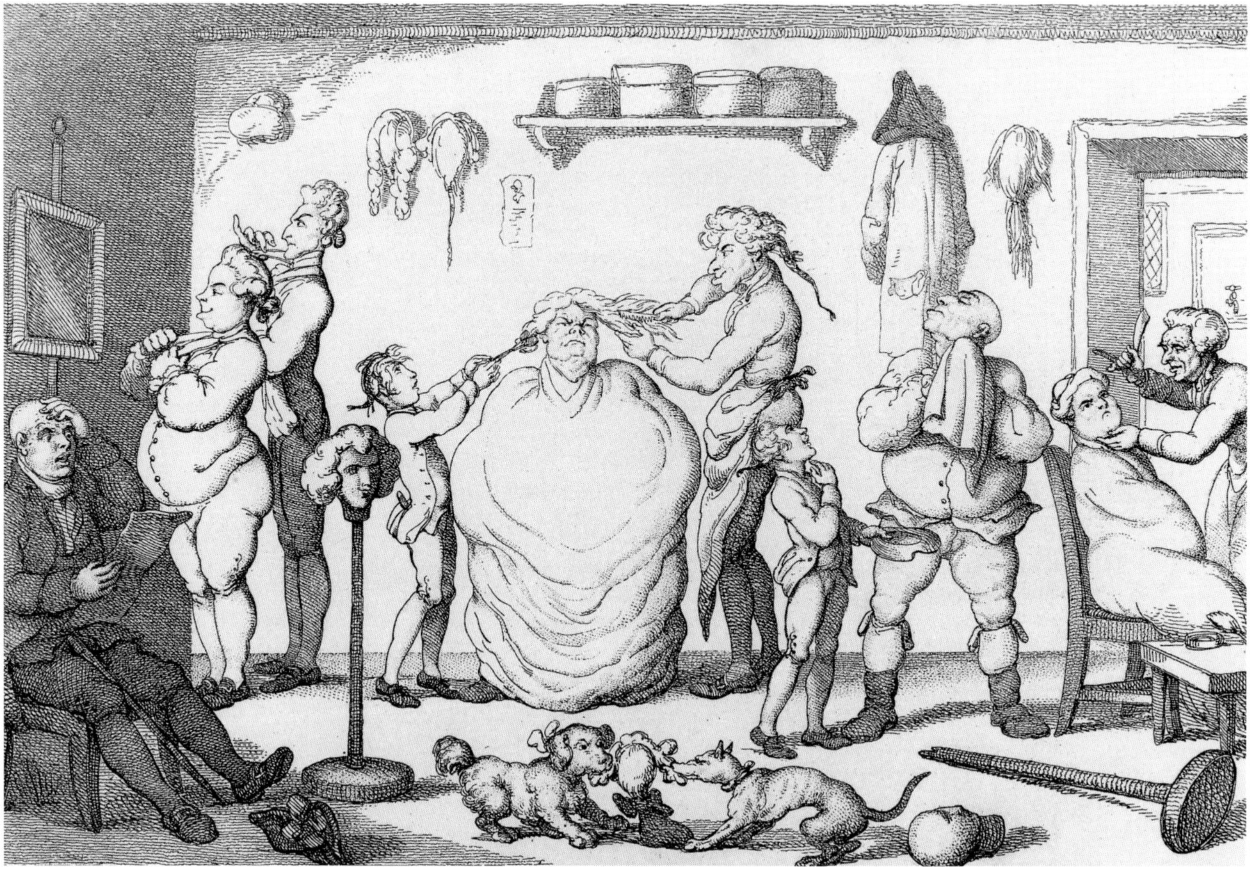

A Barbers Shop, *by Thomas Rowlandson after Bunbury. Two dogs fight over a Bag Wig*

younger members of the Bar. Hogarth is again a useful witness. His engraving *The Second Stage of Cruelty* (1751) shows four gowned lawyers emerging from an overturned coach outside Thavies Inn in Holborn, oblivious to a horse being beaten beside them. The uppermost figure is seen from behind and, instead of the formally combed frontal lappets worn by the lawyer in *The Triple Plea*, this man's wig is tied behind into two 'pigeon's wings' with a slightly shorter queue at the nape of the neck.

Various styles and names of wig are associated with the law in the later eighteenth century: broadly speaking, barristers were expected to wear Tie Wigs, attorneys Bob Wigs, and judges Full-bottoms.

An article in *The Connoisseur* of 24 April 1755 by 'Mr Town' (George Colman [1732–94] and Bonnell Thornton [1724–68]) presents a useful survey of contemporary offence against etiquette. It condemns, for example, a certain Mr Reverend Jessamy, known as 'the Beau-Parson' for the affected style of his wig: 'His very grizzle is scarce orthodox: for, though it would be open schism to wear a bag, yet his wig has always a bag-front.' Such is the fashion assumed by 'neuter somethings between male and female':

> This folly is also to be particularly condemned, when it appears in the more solemn characters of life, to which a gravity of appearance is essential; and in which the least marks of foppery seem as improper, as a physician would seem ridiculous prescribing in a bag-wig, or a serjeant pleading at the King's Bench in his own hair instead of a night-cap periwig.

Whilst in 1709 Steele had considered 'nightcap wigs' among the 'enormities' of fashion worn by 'persons that dress themselves as they please, without regard to decorum', by 1755 the same style of wig had come to embody the 'gravity of appearance' essential to the function of justice. By 1778 the 'ridiculous' impropriety of Mr Town's 'physician . . . prescribing in a bag-wig' had also come to pass, as remarked upon by Boswell (see p. 25).

William Woty, who came to London as clerk to a solicitor, published 'The Caxon' (1760) under the pseudonym of 'James Copywell of Lincolns Inn'. After praising the Caxon over the beau's 'bag-wig elate' and the 'bushy Hair . . . Of lordly Physick', Woty turns to what he calls 'the tye/Of Barrister loquacious . . . the powder'd badge/Of consequence external':

> What plaudit would he draw, if Cut or Scratch
> Debas'd his temples, and his cheek expos'd?
> But tho' the stately Tye such honour beams
> Round semi-circled Noddle . . .
> . . . the Caxon still I prize.

The fact that the shorter styles of Cut or Scratch would expose his cheek confirms that 'up to the nineteenth century [the barrister's wig] was rather fuller than at present'.

Woty goes on to refer to the larger Full-bottomed style of wig retained by judges when he writes, 'Let not the Justice, whose idea-pot*/Encircling curls keep warm, the Caxon spurn.'

A work by the playwright Richard Brinsley Sheridan (1751–1816) demonstrates that attorneys, too, wore a distinctive wig. 'You ought to be asham'd to shew your face at the Sessions,' says a character to a deceived judge in *St Patrick's Day* (1785). 'You'll be the laughing-stock of the Bench, and a bye word with all the Pigtail'd Lawyers and Bobwig Attornies.' While attorneys stopped wearing wigs when the general fashion declined in the later eighteenth century, barristers and judges have continued to wear them in court.

By the 1770s it had become the fashion to wear a Tie Wig with two or three rows of horizontal buckled curls along the back and sides of the head, a trend adopted by barristers. A portrait, probably dating from 1772, of the legal antiquary Francis Hargrave (?1741–1821), shows him as a junior barrister wearing a curled Tie Wig of this sort. Today's barristers wear a wig composed of a frizzed crown, beneath which are ranged three horizontal rows of seven cylindrical buckles, then one row of four buckles, one upright perpendicular buckle at the top of the neck, then a final row of two buckles beneath which hang two looped tails. Originally somewhat fuller in volume and size, it continued to be worn greased and powdered until the introduction of patent wigs that simulated a powdered finish.

That is, the head

This development was pioneered in the early nineteenth century by Humphrey Ravenscroft, the grandson of Thomas Ravenscroft who had founded his wig-making business in 1726. On 14 March 1822, after years of experimentation, Humphrey Ravenscroft published the patent to a Tie Wig that would finally dispense with the inconvenience of maintaining it, which involved treating it almost daily with a thick, scented ointment ('pomatum') and powder. In the words of the patent itself the white horsehair curls of this 'forensic' (in the sense of 'legal') wig

> . . . are constructed on a Principal to Supersede the Necessity for Frizzing, Curling, or Using Hard Pomatum, and for forming the Curls in a Way not to be Uncurled, and also for the Tails of the Wig not to require Tying in Dressing; and, further, the Impossibility of any Person Untying them.

The innovation was an immediate success, though it was resisted by some. According to Croake James, in his

Recollections of the Court of Common Pleas *(1834) by George Cruikshank. Barristers, Serjeants and Judges are all recognisable by their wigs*

book *Curiosities of Law and Lawyers* (1891), Sir James Alan Park (1763–1838), a Judge of the Common Pleas, 'actually refused to recognise his own son at the bar when he appeared in one of the new-fangled wigs', and though examples are documented of barristers who continued to grease and powder their wigs well into the twentieth century, the firm of Ede and Ravenscroft continues to manufacture barristers' wigs according to the pattern and method described in the 1822 patent.

When women were first called to the Bar in 1922 there was some debate as to whether their entitlement should extend to the wearing of wigs. It was suggested that they should revert to the Tudor-style biretta, a soft, cornered black cap, before a vote among certain senior judges decided the matter. In March 1922 it was decided that women barristers should in fact wear the wig 'which shall completely cover and conceal the hair'. Sikh barristers have been allowed to wear their turban instead of the wig since the 1960s.

◆◆◆

In the case of judges, their present-day court and full-dress wigs continue to incorporate elements that actually predate the general seventeenth-century fashion for wigs. A distinctive judicial costume had emerged by the fifteenth century. Judges wore a black skull-cap, which was worn over a close-fitting white cap known as the coif (and also, briefly, as the 'houf'), which indicated their status as serjeants-at-law, the medieval Order of the Coif from whose members judges were chosen. The coif covered the wearer's brow and ears and was secured under the chin, the total effect somewhat resembling a modern balaclava helmet. Langland's *Vision of Piers Plowman* (*c.*1370) refers to a 'serjaunt' wearing 'a silke houve', but Richard Hooker's *Of the Lawes of Ecclesiasticall Politie* of 1597 mentions a 'linnen coife' as 'an ornament which only sergeants at law doe weare'. A symbolic reminder of this may be seen in the indentation in the crown of today's Judge's Bench wig (see pp 49-50 below). By this time the judge's costume had come to include a third item of headgear, the *pileus quadratus* or biretta, mentioned above. This limp, black, usually cornered cap was first depicted on the tomb of Serjeant William Rudhall, who died in 1530. Monumental effigies and brasses depict judges wearing coif, skull-cap and cornered cap through the sixteenth century, and although some of these do not show the cornered cap, it had become a standard part of the judge's costume by 1635.

On 4 June 1635 judges signed a set of rules concerning the dress of judges and serjeants, which includes the rule that 'judges in term-time are to sit at Westminster in the courts . . . wearing their velvet caps and coifs of lawn and cornered caps'. The white coif of the serjeant and the black skull-cap, worn by judges and barristers, began steadily to diminish in size from around the early seventeenth century. The coif came to resemble in shape the skull-cap that almost covered it, and the two items evolved into a single black skull-cap with a lining of white lawn (the coif) slightly protruding beneath the brim. The cornered cap ceased to be worn when wigs were introduced except on formal occasions when it was laid over the wig. By Victorian times it had come to be associated with the passing of a death sentence.

While the fashion for wigs swiftly permeated the legal profession, some older judges, such as Sir Matthew Hale (1609–76) and Sir Thomas Street (1626–96), continued to wear their own hair. Those judges who adopted the natural-coloured Full-bottom Wig, and the later fashion for wearing it powdered, continued to wear the white coif and black skull-cap in a single piece attached to the back of their wigs. While the coif-lined skull-cap just covers the ears in portraits of serjeants from the middle of the seventeenth century, there is in the parish church of Mottram-in-Longdendale, Cheshire, the carved effigy of one Serjeant Reginald Bretland (died 1703) wearing a smaller circular coif and cap approximately the size of the back of his head. A painting in London's National Portrait Gallery, by Benjamin Ferrers (died 1732), of the Court of Chancery about 1718–25 includes the detail of a serjeant seen from behind. The serjeant is depicted in a wig very similar to that shown in Hogarth's *The Triple Plea* of the same period: the two sides or 'lappets' of the Full-bottom drape over his shoulders, while a small tail or queue extends a few inches down his back. Ferrers's serjeant wears on the back of his wig a spade-shaped black velvet cap which entirely obscures the white coif beneath it. The white edging symbolising the coif is visible beneath the velvet cap on the wigs of two other figures in the painting and the coif and cap

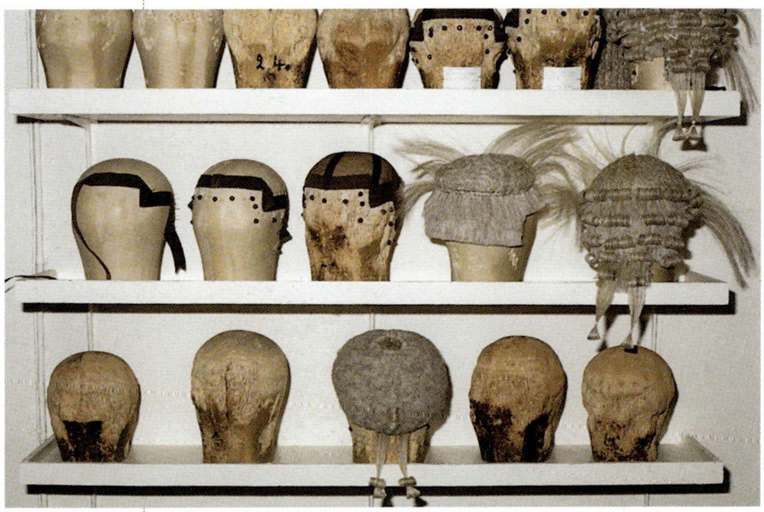

Wood blocks on shelves in Ede and Ravenscroft's workroom with wigs at different stages of manufacture

The Bench *by William Hogarth (1758), showing judges still wearing long Full-bottomed Wigs of late seventeenth-century proportions*

are slightly larger than those on Bretland's effigy and with straighter edges.

When the vogue for smaller, more stylised Tie Wigs came to be adopted by younger members of the Bar in the 1730s, judges displayed the same reluctance to change as had some in the 1660s and retained instead the Full-bottomed style 'formally combed all before' that Gay described in 1713. Large wigs such as these had two effects on the 'velvet caps and coifs of lawn and cornered caps' decreed to be worn by judges in the 1635 regulations. First, the already stylised coif and skull-cap diminished still further in size; secondly, the black cornered cap was carried in the hand on ceremonial occasions, being only worn rarely over the wig..

Two further works by Hogarth from the 1750s well illustrate this larger style of judicial wig and the corresponding diminution of the coif and skull-cap worn at its crown. His engraving *Paul before Felix* (1751) – a parody of his own painting of the same subject (1748) – casts its biblical subject in partly modern dress. Paul's prosecuting counsel, 'a certain orator named Tertullus, who informed the governor against Paul' (Acts 24:1) is 'arrayed in the habit of an English serjeant-at-law . . . irritated almost to madness by Paul's lecture on the supremacy of divine over earthly justice, he tears his brief: this, a devil . . . is carefully picking up and joining the remnants together.' Tertullus the serjeant wears a shoulder-length, formally combed white Full-bottomed Wig, on whose crown sits a small, circular patch of black, edged in white.

A black skull-cap, though without the white edging, is clearly visible on the heads of three of the four somnolent judges of the Court of Common Pleas depicted in Hogarth's *The Bench* (1758). Each of the two central figures wears a flamboyant white Full-bottom with the lappets reaching down to the chest. On the left sits a third judge in profile, his head all but hidden by a massive, dark-coloured Full-bottomed Wig which was the ordinary lay style of William III's time. In the small painted version of the engraving in the Fitzwilliam Museum, Cambridge, this wig is of a very dark, slightly reddish brown. On the right in the engraving (the left of the painting) slumps a judge wearing a Full-bottom which is white in the painting and a darker grey in the engraving, of the same great size, whose 'Encircling curls', as Woty put it, surround the man's whole face.

Judges were wearing such voluminous styles of wig as late as the nineteenth century. A portrait of Sir Charles Abbot, Chief Justice of the King's Bench 1818–32, shows him wearing a wig of the same dimensions as his predecessor in *The Bench*, though with a trimmer crown. A satirical print from 1823 shows a bald judge being fitted for a new Full-bottom of much the same size. An anonymous article from 1877, entitled 'Judicial Costume', notes that 'until recently the early full-bottoms made of thin horsehair from the manes were greased and powdered every week or two. Latterly patent wigs have come into use, made of thick white horsehair and worn without powder since they simulate the powdered effect.'

In fact, the patent to the first 'new and improved Full-Bottom Wig' dates from nearly fifty years before. Following the success of his barrister's wig in 1822, Humphrey Ravenscroft devoted himself to the manufacture of an equivalent Full-bottom, and published his results on 1 January 1835. Retailing at twelve guineas, Ravenscroft's 'new and improved' design 're-modelled and executed on an entirely new principle' was advertised as follows:

> . . . the Flaps or Wings having the same uniformity of curl as the Body of the Wig, and by their peculiar construction they retain the powder and pomatum, which will not fall out in wearing, neither will they soil or powder the silk gowns or robes in the manner the common Full-Bottom Wigs usually do . . . The Patentee . . . will guarantee that the Hair of the Full-Bottom Wig shall retain the same uniformity of curl all over, so long as they can possibly be worn and dressed; and also, that the powder and pomatum will not fall through the Flaps or Wings; and, what is of infinite advantage, they will not in the slightest degree oppose the organ of hearing.

As the anonymous author of 'Judicial Costume' admitted in 1877, many 'modern' judges remained deaf to such innovation and continued to use grease and flour on their old-style wigs.

Wigs were resisted by senior judges when the fashion first arose; then the Full-bottom was retained as the fashion dwindled to smaller styles; then, when the fashion disappeared from general use, it was only judges, barristers, clergymen and coachmen, the holders of a few civic offices and (for a short time) doctors who retained it; the introduction of patent wigs in the second quarter of the nineteenth century was in turn resisted by the judiciary. With the exception of State coachmen it is largely only members of the legal profession who retain the fashion to this day. A judge's full-dress wig today has a so-called 'doormat' effect from its twenty-odd rows of tightly wound curls. Judges wear such wigs on ceremonial occasions, as do QCs, who also wear

Head of a Judge *subtitled* A Representation of the Ice in the Fountain of Garden Court, Temple on 26 January 1795, *published 16 March 1795 by Laurie &Whittle, 53 Fleet Street*

The Speaker of the House of Commons. 1861 photograph of the Rt Hon. J .E. Denison (1800–73), Speaker 1857–72, created Viscount Ossington 1872, wearing Full-bottomed Wig, beaver three-cornered hat, court coat and robe of black satin damask trimmed with gold

them when pleading in the House of Lords. The Lord Chancellor wears one when sitting on the Woolsack in the Lords, while the Speaker of the House of Commons also wore a Full-bottom wig when Parliament sat, though the practice was suspended when the Right Hon. Betty Boothroyd was appointed Speaker in 1992. Her successor, the Right Hon. Michael Martin, the 156th Speaker, has chosen not to wear a wig.

Judges do not try cases wearing the ceremonial Full-bottom, but the wigs they wear do still bear a symbolic trace of medieval dress in the small indentation on the crown, which is a reference to the coif, as described below. Around 1770, many judges had at last taken to wearing smaller wigs for ordinary occasions in court, adopting the short frizzed Bob Wig with a single vertical buckle on the base at the back, and a horizontal buckle on each of the two short tails that hang behind. At the crown of this wig, as a mark of distinction from the general fashion, was worn a diminished representation of the judge's black skull-cap and serjeant-at-law's coif. By Victorian times this had shrunk to a small circular patch of black silk with a crimped hem of white lawn with a diameter of about two inches. The Judicature Act 1873, which came into force in 1876, stated that new judges were not required to take

The Lord Chief Justice 1989. Lord Lane, Lord Chief Justice (1980–92), in Full-bottomed Wig, scarlet robe and the Lord Chief Justice's Collar of SS

or have taken the degree of serjeant-at-law. Thereafter no new judges were serjeants and so the coif was no longer worn, although in memory of the coif's medieval origin the judge's short undress wig retained, and retains

The three types of legal wig (from left to right): Full-bottomed, Bar, and Bench or Tie Wig. Also depicted is a wig box

to this day, a small circular depression at its crown where the coif was once worn. This wig is now known as the Judge's Bench or Tye Wig. It is frizzed all over with no rows of buckles or curls and has two small ties of horsehair at the back. (In having these ties it resembles the barrister's Tie, or Bar, Wig, whereas the judge's Full-bottomed Wig has no queue.)

'Who would have supposed,' wrote John Campbell (1799–1861), subsequently Lord Campbell the Lord Chancellor, in *The Lives of the Lord Chancellors* (1845), 'that this grotesque ornament, fit only for an African Chief, would be considered indispensably necessary for the administration of justice in the middle of the nineteenth century?'

Yet, as an accessory which started by displaying its wearer's social and professional standing – even if some did consider it 'grotesque' – it came to inspire respect, lending to its wearer a certain formal gravity, and it still bestows upon today's legal proceedings the necessarily formal dignity of justice. In the twenty-first century it has become a symbol of impartiality, helping to make the administration of justice impersonal.

From Noble Robe to Ignominious Habit: The Barrister's Gown

Perhaps the law has a particular ability to recognise, albeit slowly, a fashion item that especially suits the profession's dignity, for in much the same way as, in the late eighteenth century, the legal profession retained the wig when the general fashion for it declined, lawyers in the fourteenth century became distinguished from those in other professions by continuing to wear the long *tunica* generally worn by men until the mid-1300s. There is no evidence to suggest that before then the costume of members of the legal profession below the rank of serjeant-at-law (the most senior barristers) was regulated. Until the later part of the fourteenth century, both judges and serjeants-at-law wore a wide-sleeved knee-length tabard called a collobium; judges then adopted a different costume, a brief history of which is given later (p. 65).

In one of the earliest extant illustrations of barristers, from a thirteenth-century legal treatise, *Judicium Essoniorum*, they are depicted wearing the *tunica*, a plain, sleeved ankle-length surcoat, closed at the front. The costume historian J. R. Planché (Somerset Herald 1866–80) relates that around the year 1340 there was a general reaction against the fashion for these long coats in favour of a shorter, tighter-fitting style – lawyers, however, continued to wear the long robe.

In the centuries that follow, examples of this garment are to be found specifically in relation to the legal profession. Sir John Fortescue, for instance, Chief Justice of the King's Bench, refers to it in his *De Laudibus Legum Angliae* (1471), and it is illustrated in a number of fifteenth-century monumental brasses. There is at Trottescliffe, Kent, a brass of William Crofton, who died in 1480 and is described as *'bacallarius Juris Civilis et legis peritus ac Collega de Greysyn* [Gray's Inn]'. It shows him

The Court of Chancery c.1460, depicting the Chancellor and Master of the Robes in Scarlet with three Serjeants at the Bar wearing coifs

The Court of King's Bench c.1460. Five judges wearing coifs preside in scarlet robes

in a pleated tunica, edged at the collar, cuffs and ankle-length hem with what appears to be fur, and secured at the waist with an elaborate belt from which hangs a large purse or bag.

In the possession of the Inner Temple are four coloured pictures, dating from about 1460, of the Courts of Chancery, the King's Bench, the Common Pleas, and the Exchequer, from a manuscript abridgement of the law. These Whaddon Hall illuminations (so-called because they were found at Whaddon Hall, Buckinghamshire) vividly reveal that the barrister's belted tunica was parti-coloured in blue-and-mustard and green-and-blue with diagonal stripes. While the serjeants-at-law in the pictures – identifiable from their white coif – wear a cape-like shoulder-piece with the cowl of the hood draped at the shoulders, the long robe (shown from back and front) worn by the barristers is exactly as in William Crofton's brass, though without the waist-purse. Both serjeants' and barristers' robes are parti-coloured – that is, divided vertically and of two different colours; and one of the colours is usually rayed – that is, made of cloth of one colour with contrasting parallel lines or rays, through the cloth, of another colour. The serjeants are shown with vertical stripes on the rayed side of their robes, and the barristers with diagonal. Diagonal lines appear on the

The Court of Exchequer c.1460 presided over by the Barons of the Exchequer, the Chief Baron in scarlet robes and a scarlet, turban-like hood

collobium of the serjeants.

In the early Tudor period the long robe that closed at the front came to be replaced in general fashion by a long open gown, and monumental brasses from the period reveal that barristers followed this fashion. The brass at Hempstead, Essex, of William Mordaunt of the Middle Temple (died 1518) – admittedly not a barrister but Chief Prothonotary of the Common Pleas – well illustrates the evolution of this garment from the tunica shown in Crofton's brass of forty years before. Mordaunt wears an ankle-length gown which, as J. H. Baker, the leading historian of legal dress, comments, 'seems not to be wholly open in front', with voluminous, fur-edged sleeves and a broad fur lapel spreading over the shoulders.

In the same period, the vivid colours of the barristers' parti-coloured and rayed robes were replaced by more sombre, muted ones as documented in two wills of Readers of the Middle Temple. Robert Pynkney's will, dated 20 May 1508, mentions a crimson gown edged in fur – '*meam togam de crimsyn pemlatam cum furrys*' – and a mulberry-coloured (purple-red) gown with a lining of light brown damask – '*unam togam de murrey lyned w*th *tawny damaske*'. That of Thomas Jubbes, dated 3 July 1528, mentions a 'blacke gowne furr^{d} w^{t} foynes [foin is beech marten fur], my gowne lyn^{d} w^{t} damaske and my gowne lyn^{d} w^{t} chamblett' (camlet, a type of cloth) and

The Court of Common Pleas c.1460 with the Chief Justice and six Puisne judges presiding

also a 'russet gowne furr^{d} w^{t} foxe'. Jubbes's bequest of the latter gown to his servant demonstrates that the long gown was 'not yet a prescribed uniform' exclusively for lawyers; 'the only requirement so far was sobriety' of clothing, as Professor Baker remarks, and a number of regulations were from 1531 onwards issued to members of all four Inns of Court to this effect. In 1557, for example, it was agreed by all the Inns that 'none of the companions, except knights or benchers, should wear in their doublets or hose any light colours, except scarlet and crimson, nor wear any upper velvet cap, or any scarf, or wings, i.e. folds of cloth on the sleeves, in their gowns', and in the same year there was a regulation against cloaks so that gowns were encouraged, and then, between 1580 and 1600, ordered to be worn.

By the beginning of the seventeenth century a plain style of full-length gown, probably in black, had emerged as the appropriate pattern for members of the Inns of Court. The voluminous sleeves shown in Mordaunt's monumental brass from 1518 evolved into hollow glove-sleeves through which the arms were passed. The slits, and sometimes the edging of the glove-sleeves, seem to have been decorated with strips or 'welts' of velvet or 'doctor's lace' – the black, woven braid-like ornament still used on academic gowns – though any further decoration was disapproved of, as Mr Secondary Kempe of the King's Bench noted in 1602:

> . . . in tymes past the counsellors wore gowns faced with satten, and some with yellowe cotten, and the benchers with jennet furre; now they are come to that pride and fanstasticknes that every one must have a velvet face, and some soe tricked with lace that Justice Wray [Christopher Wray, 1524–92] in his tyme spake to such an odd counsellor in this manner ... 'Get you from the barre, or I will put you from the barr for your folish pride.'

It should be noted, however, that sixteenth-century lawyers were required to wear gowns in accordance with the regulations of the Inns of Court where they studied, rather as Oxford and Cambridge undergraduates once were, and that the same gowns were worn for appearances at the Bar.

The monumental brass at Epping in Essex, of Thomas Palmer, utter barrister of the Middle Temple, who died in 1621, shows him in an ankle-length gown, which he wears with a ruff around his neck with two raised peaks on the shoulders. The brass clearly illustrates the 'welts' or velvet trim of the by now increasingly standard barrister's gown. According to Sir Henry

Chauncy (1632–1719), who was called to the Bar of the Middle Temple in 1656, 'Utter Baristers' were 'adorn'd with a Noble Robe, fac'd down before, guarded with two welts of Velvet on the Sleeves extending from the Shoulder to the Elbow, and another on the border of it.'

Full ceremonial dress for a QC includes breeches, black silk stockings and black patent leather shoes with cut steel buckles. (Photo: Garlinda Birkbeck)

These double welts of velvet running vertically on the upper part of the sleeve were the really distinctive feature of the old Bar gown. Between 1637, when counsellors were ordered by the Privy Council to appear in 'their gownes according to theire places', and 1685, this was the standard pattern of the barrister's gown, as a number of monumental brasses show. Readers in the Inns of Court, as compared to utter barristers, wore a gown with a velvet welt on the back. In the Restoration period, gowns with velvet facings, lace and tufts, came to be appropriated exclusively to Law Officers of the Crown and King's Counsel.

Previous generations of legal historians have linked the design of the modern barrister's gown to the periods of mourning that followed the deaths of Queen Mary, in 1694, and of Queen Anne, in 1714. However, J. H. Baker argues that it derives from the style of mourning gown assumed by the Bar following the death of Charles II in 1685 and retained, despite early opposition, ever since. Notwithstanding the lack of definitive pictorial evidence, Baker cites the crucial testimony of three late-seventeenth-century writers, including Sir Henry Chauncy, whose description of the 'Noble Robe' worn during Charles II's reign is quoted above. Sir Henry Chauncy continues as follows:

> . . . it seems very ominous that these learned Men should now decline this Noble Robe, and wear a scandalous Livery which resemble those that Bearers usually wear at Funerals, as though the Law lay a dying: However it is greatly hoped, That that worthy Patron of the *Law*, Sir *John Holt,* the present Lord Chief Justice, will thoroughly reform this ill practice, and that none of the Reverend Sages of the Law will suffer those Gentlemen to share in the profit and advantage of that Profession which they scandalize by devesting it of that Ancient Robe, and introducing an ignominious Habit in the room of it.

Sir John Holt (1642–1710) served as Lord Chief Justice of the King's Bench from 1689 till his death. That the change Chauncy describes, from 'Noble Robe' to 'ignominious Habit', dates from the death of Charles II in 1685 and not from that of Queen Mary in 1694 is borne out by two further documents. The first of these is an entry dated 30 October 1697 in *A Brief Historicall Relation of State Affairs from September 1678 to April 1714* (printed 1854) compiled by the annalist and

Queen's Counsel in full ceremonial dress of a Full-bottomed Wig, silk gown, lace stock and cuffs. (Photo: Garlinda Birkbeck)

bibliographer Narcissus Luttrell (1657–1732). It states that 'Yesterday [i.e. the first day of the Michaelmas Term in the legal calendar] the lord cheif justice Holt ordered all baristers to appear next term in their proper gowns, and not in mourning ones, as *they have done since the death of King Charles*; otherwise will not hear them.' Luttrell later notes that Holt's order was observed, and that on the first day of the following term 'the baristers appeared at the kings bench in such gowns as they wore before the death of King Charles the 2d ... and 'tis said the other courts will follow their example.'

The second document is a manuscript account of the same events by the antiquary James Wright (1643–1713), who became a barrister in the Middle Temple in 1675: 'The Lord Chief Justice Holt caused most of those who practised before him at the King's Bench to resume the wearing of the old-fashion'd Bar-Gowns . . . which sort of Gowns had been utterly disused for many years past.'

'The order did not stand for long,' comments Baker, and it may well be that the publication three years later of Chauncy's hopes that 'Sir John Holt . . . will thoroughly reform this ill practice' alludes to the enduring reluctance among barristers to return to the more expensive and more uncomfortable 'Noble Robe'.

At Abingdon in Northamptonshire, the full-length effigy of William Thursby, bencher of the Middle Temple, dating from shortly after his death in 1701, clearly shows the bell-shaped sleeves, buttoned and taped at the elbow, the pleated shoulders, and lighter 'stuff' material of the mourning gown, which in a somewhat shorter style remains the fashion of the modern Bar. It does not, however, show the most distinctive feature of the 1685 gown to have survived – the 'two curious appendages of cloth' that James Derriman describes in *Pageantry of the Law* (1955), 'attached to the left shoulder and hanging down the garment':

> One of these appendages is shaped rather like a violin sliced in two length-wise, attached to the back of the gown along the straight edge, the smaller (upper) part being closed off from the lower one, which is open at the bottom end. The second appendage is a long strip of cloth hanging down the front of the gown.

This fold of material at the back of the gown has also been likened to a 'cloven tongue' and to 'the wattles of a cock or turkey' (the word 'wallet' is said to derive from the word 'wattle', meaning bag). The shape, however, as Baker comments, 'is not easy to describe in words' nor easy to draw clearly.

Viewed from behind, on a modern barrister's gown this fold of cloth is perhaps best described as a roughly triangular, folded flap, the apex uppermost, with the diagonals about ten inches long; it has a horizontal base, not sewn shut, which measures about six inches across. A shorter, narrower, tapering flap, about eight inches long, shaped rather like a modern tie, is folded over from the right, covering a third of the triangle's width and leaving uncovered about two inches at the base of the triangle. The whole fold of material at the back of the gown is attached at around the level of the shoulder-blade to a strip of cloth about two inches wide, which hangs in front of the wearer to just below waist-level. The precise nature and origin of this double-folded, triangular flap of material has long exercised costume historians.

One of the most enduring theories is that it represents a convenient purse or bag. This suggestion was firmly in place as early as 1795. 'It is certain,' comments a correspondent to the *Gentleman's Magazine* in July of that year, 'that many parts of our professional *res vestiariae*. . . were at first of use; e.g. our serjeant's patch was to hide the tonsure; the tippet behind a barrister's gown was a wallet to carry his breviates in.' The serjeant-at-law's 'patch' was in fact a small version of the medieval coif which originally covered the wearer's crown and ears. The author's confident description of the folded material behind a barrister's gown as a 'wallet' for 'breviates' (i.e. lawyer's briefs) is similarly fanciful, though variants upon the theory have become a popular myth.

Historically barristers did not technically receive explicit payment for their work. Since their fees were *honoraria* (so the theory goes), their clients might surreptitiously slip money into the purse carried on their gowns, literally behind their back, 'without ruffling the susceptibilities or offending the dignity of the learned counsellor', in the words of J. S. Udal, writing in the periodical *Notes and Queries* in 1887. Another version holds that, since the barrister could not see the exact amount being paid him, whether large or small, he would not allow the verve with which he pleaded his case to be influenced. A more prosaic theory holds that the barrister's performance in court would once have relied upon a client's constant topping-up of the wallet behind him, worn at the back so as not to disturb his rhetorical flow. The theory has even been advanced into the field of literary criticism. In Shakespeare's *Troilus and Cressida* (1602), Ulysses says that 'Time hath . . . a wallet at his back, / Wherein he puts alms for oblivion.' 'It may

Three barristers in Bar Wigs and gowns. The wigs are of white horsehair as patented by Humphrey Ravenscroft in 1822

be worth noting,' comments one editor, 'that a barrister's robe still includes a small bag which hangs behind the shoulder' – a suggestion apparently supported by the fact that the play was written for private performance at the Inns of Court.

The second long-standing theory to account for the cloth 'wallet' and 'strip' on the barrister's gown is that it 'derived from the medieval fashion of the *chaperon*', the hood-like band of cloth, also known as the *chausse,* which lay at the shoulder and to which was attached a padded cap, the *bourrelet,* which hung behind the wearer's back when not required. It is true that one of the barristers depicted in the Whaddon Hall illumination of the Court of Exchequer apparently wears such an appendage over the left shoulder of his parti-coloured robe; and that the chaperon became a distinctive feature of French advocates in medieval times.

Yet, against this evidence, as Baker again convincingly argues, should be set the documented fact that in Tudor and Stuart times the hood was the defining garment of the serjeant-at-law, as a judge's address to such men in 1521 demonstrates: 'so yow by this tabard and hode are known from the resideue which be studens of the lawe'. Among this 'resideue', of course, must be counted barristers. Though the matter is complicated by the absence of rear views in monumental brasses of sixteenth- and seventeenth-century barristers, it seems notable that Sir Henry Chauncy's otherwise full description of the old-fashioned 'Noble Robe' makes no mention of a hood. In fact it seems clear that it was Chauncy's 'ignominious Habit', the mourning gown introduced after the death of Charles II, that first included a hood, not as a symbol of rank in the legal profession as it had been for serjeants but rather as part of customary mourning dress.

The true origin of the 'wallet' at the back of the barrister's gown is vividly illustrated among the 32 plates illustrating the *Funeral Procession of Sir Philip Sidney* (1587), 'first drawne and invented' by Thomas Lant (later Portcullis Pursuivant 1588, Windsor Herald 1597) and engraved by Theodore de Bry. In Plate 15, the five named heralds bearing 'the Hatchment and dignitye of his knighthoode' wear full hoods over their heads, which taper at the back into long tails known as 'liripipes'. Plate 11 depicts twelve 'Esquiers of his kindred and frends'. All of them wear the tall brimmed hats known as sugar-loaves, ankle-length gowns, and over their left shoulder a diminutive version of the full mourning hood worn by the heralds, held in place by a thin strip of material hanging down to thigh-level. Their costume conforms

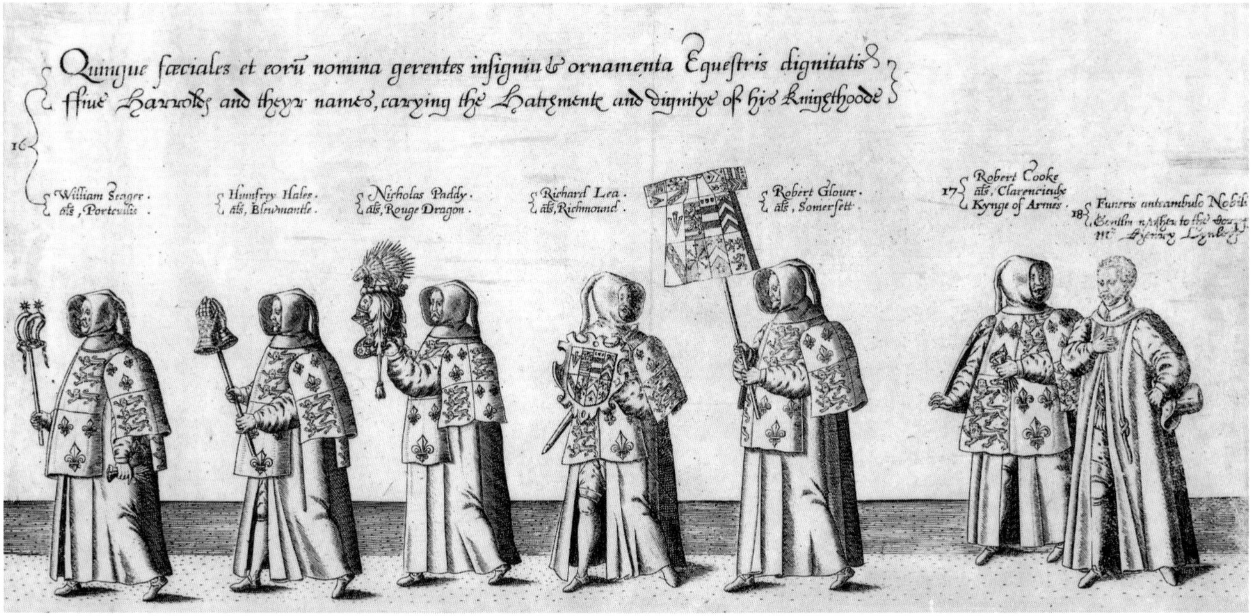
Quinque fæciales et eorũ nomina gerentes insignia & ornamenta Equestris dignitatis
ffiue Harrolds and theyr names, caryinge the Hatchmente and dignitye of his Knighthoode
16
William Seager. als, Portcullis.
Humfrey Hales. als, Blewmantle.
Nicholas Paddy. als, Rouge Dragon.
Richard Lea. als, Richmound.
Robert Glouer. als, Somersett.
17
Robert Cooke als, Clarencieulx Kynge of Armes.
18
Funeris antambulo

11

Funeral of Sir Philip Sidney *(1587)*. (Top left*) Heralds wearing full mourning hoods tapering into long tails known as liripipes.* (Bottom left*) 'Esquiers of his kindred and friends' wearing mourning hoods over their left shoulders.* (Above*) Members of the Grocers' Company with mourning hoods over their left shoulders, the liripipes hanging down in front*

to the funeral prescriptions made in an early sixteenth-century document that gentlemen wear gowns 'with hoodes on there left shoulderes'.

According to P. Cunnington and C. Lucas in *Costumes for Births, Marriages and Deaths* (1992):

> In all hoods the apex was extended into a long tail or liripipe, now confusingly called 'tippet'. Hoods not worn on the head appear from drawings to have been vestigial in type, rather like a reduced medieval chaperon (itself derived from the medieval hood). Like the livery company's and the Garter Knights' hoods, it was slung over the shoulder or round the neck by its tippet.

Plate 23 of de Bry's engraving depicts fourteen members of 'the Company of Grocers in theyr livery', all of them wearing caps and gowns and all of them wearing over their left shoulder this 'reduced medieval chaperon' – a bag-like appendage at the back and the thin strip of material in front, the liripipe, which most of them hold in their left hand. Though the drawing of these diminutive livery hoods seems to anticipate the 'wallet theory' outlined above, the mouth of the 'bag' corresponding to the front of the hood, the true prototype for the waist-length strip of cloth and folded flap of material of the modern barrister's gown, derives from the hood *specifically worn by gentlemen as a sign of mourning*, as illustrated in de Bry's engraving of the 'Esquiers'.

Many nineteenth-century contributors to the debate in the journal *Notes and Queries* claim its origins in 'the ancient hood' and assume an unbroken continuity from medieval times. In the early sixteenth century, however, barristers did not wear hoods. Rather, as we have seen, the 'Noble Robe' Chauncy described came to be replaced on the death of Charles II by an 'ignominious Habit' which itself included the funeral custom of the mourning hood.

In 1685 members of the Bar temporarily adopted, then permanently retained, a style of gown that incorporated over the left shoulder the vestigial hood and liripipe of traditional mourning costume. 'Why the *left* shoulder was insisted upon is obscure,' comments Baker, 'whereas the judges and serjeants wore their scarlet hoods cast over the right shoulder.' The obscurity is possibly explained by the terms of Baker's argument. According to the rules of judicial dress drawn up in 1635, the so-called casting-hoods of serjeants-at-law and judges were to be worn over the right shoulder as a sign of their 'temporal dignity'; if worn 'on the left side only, the Judges resemble Priests'. The wearing of the mourning hood over the left shoulder probably observes the age-old association of the left or 'sinister' side with ill luck, the setting sun and death, matters spiritual rather than temporal and more appropriate therefore to the jurisdiction of the priest rather than the judge. The vestigial hood of the barrister's gown is worn on the left to distinguish its spiritual origins in mourning from the temporal authority vested in the judge's hood worn on the right.

It is Charles II who emerges as the key figure in the history of legal costume – the style of the barrister's gown itself with the 'wallet' at its back representing the hood of the mourning gown assumed in 1685 in honour of the king whose restoration to the throne had first introduced into the realm the fashion for wigs which to this day remains an indispensable feature of the Bar.

Gown, Hood and Mantle: The Judge's Habit

In contrast to the sombre gowns of barristers, judges' robes have retained, at least in their ceremonial form, some of their medieval colour. As noted earlier, judges once wore the same dress as serjeants-at-law: fourteenth-century illustrations show them wearing a collobium, or knee-length tabard, with wide sleeves over long robes and with a coif on their heads.

In the later part of that century judges gave up this costume in favour of a long robe with a cloak and a hood (described more fully below); now only serjeants wore the collobium. In *The Order of Serjeants-at-Law* (1984), J. H. Baker quotes Sir John Fortescue, who became a serjeant in 1438 and a judge in 1442, describing the distinction between the judge's and serjeant's dress in *De Laudibus Legum Angliae* (1471).

> While he was a serjeant at law he wore a long robe like a priest's, with a furred hood spread about his shoulders, and above that a tabard [*collobium*] with two lapels, such as doctors of law are wont to use in certain universities, together with the coif . . . But on being made a judge he is dressed in a cloak [*clamis*], fastened on the right shoulder, in place of the tabard. The other ornaments of a serjeant are retained, save that a judge does not use rayed or parti-coloured garments (as a serjeant can), and his hood is furred only with miniver (whereas a serjeant's hood is always lined with white lambskin).

Fortescue described the serjeant's coif as the first and foremost of the marks of dress with which serjeants are distinguished at their creation, and the poet John Gower (died 1418) in *Mirour de l'Omme* is probably referring to a coifing ceremony when he wrote that an apprentice competent in pleading could apply to have the coif put on his head and be called a serjeant.

The serjeant's tabard became increasingly a ceremonial garment and was last worn in the eighteenth century. After the Judicature Act 1873 came into force in 1876 no judges of the new Supreme Court of

Judicature were required to be serjeants. The last serjeant to be created was Nathaniel Lindley in May 1875 prior to becoming a Judge of the Common Pleas. Non-judicial serjeants just missed surviving into the twentieth century, as F. L. Spinks (1816–99), the last serjeant at the English Bar, died on 27 December 1899.

In the late fourteenth century, when judges gave up wearing the collobium, they replaced it with a cloak or mantle, fastened on the right shoulder, and a hood over a long robe. As J. H. Baker remarks in *The Order of Serjeants-at-Law*, 'The long gown, hood and mantle have been the full-dress habit of English judges ever since.'

The mantle was put on over the hood, the tail of which was pulled out. It was about six inches shorter than the long robe, which had an opening at the front, which was extended in the sixteenth century down to the waist. There was no standard practice as to the wearing of a belt, but before 1600 a plain black girdle knotted in front became a regular part of a judge's costume and remains so as a broad black sash. Between about 1615 and 1625 the judges stopped fastening the mantle on the right shoulder and fastened it centrally, beneath the chin; it was folded back so that the long robe

His Honour Judge Samuels, QC. A circuit judge in normal judicial dress and Bench Wig

was more visible, and in the course of the seventeenth century the mantle became shorter, resembling a cape

His Honour Judge Samuels, QC in full ceremonial dress including Full-bottomed Wig

rather than a cope. While the mantle became shorter in the seventeenth century, the hood became larger.

From the late fourteenth century, judges had winter and summer robes. The winter robes were lined with miniver (white stoat fur), and the summer robes with taffeta or sarsenet. Records of the late fourteenth and early fifteenth centuries describe the summer robes as green and the winter robes as violet. Pictorial evidence from the fifteenth century shows judges wearing scarlet robes; as the dye was expensive these were probably reserved for what came to be known as Red Letter Days, such as certain religious festivals and, more recently, the Sovereign's Birthday. The last mention of green robes is in 1534; thereafter judges wore scarlet or violet, both of which would have had summer and winter linings. In 1635 the judges issued regulations on dress, allowing judges to sit in either violet or black, with hoods of the same colours and linings dependent on the time of the year, while scarlet robes were worn at criminal trials, on circuit, and on certain saints' days, with linings, once again, depending on the time of year. The present rule is that black is only worn in winter, with miniver facing, and violet in summer, with silk facing.

In addition to the formal dress worn by judges when sitting in Westminster Hall, a less formal dress was adopted. This involved removing the mantle and hood and wearing a black scarf around the neck; the hood was then worn not over the head but around the neck and over the scarf. When hoods became larger it was no longer practical to wear them in this way and an unlined casting-hood was worn on the right shoulder, suspended by its liripipe or tail, obscuring the scarf. The 1635 rules state that the casting-hood could only be worn with the scarf, which is sometimes called a tippet, and they only refer to a scarlet casting-hood. The less formal dress was laid down in 1635 for civil trials, though in the eighteenth century judges on circuit in civil trials began to wear a plain black silk gown, and scarlet in trials involving the Crown. After the Judicature Act of 1875 judges reverted to wearing the black and violet robes with scarlet casting hoods when trying civil cases on circuit.

At present the full dress with hood and mantle is worn on State occasions such as the State Opening of Parliament, the first day of Michaelmas term, which is the start of the legal year, on Red Letter Days such as the Queen's Birthday and various Saints' Days. On the few occasions when a mantle is worn by judges the Lord Justices of Appeal wear a black damask robe trimmed with gold, and a similar robe is worn by the Lord Chancellor and the Master of the Rolls on State

The Hon. Mr Justice Blackburne. A High Court Judge in normal judicial dress, including Bench Wig

The Hon. Mr. Justice Blackburne in full ceremonial dress including Full-bottomed Wig

occasions. A single judge of the Queen's Bench Division when trying criminal cases wears a scarlet robe trimmed with fur or silk according to the season, and a scarf, girdle and casting hood. A judge of the same Division trying civil cases wears – except on Red Letter Days when he wears the same as a judge trying criminal cases – a black robe trimmed with fur, black scarf and scarlet casting hood in the Michaelmas and Hilary terms, and a purple cloth robe trimmed with silk, black scarf and scarlet casting hood during the Easter and Trinity terms (i.e. during the summer). All other judges of the Supreme Court wear plain black silk or stuff gowns in court. County Court Judges since 1919 have worn a violet cloth robe with lilac silk facings and cuffs, a lilac casting hood across the shoulder and a black girdle around the waist. In 1937 a violet cloth hood with facings was introduced for ceremonial occasions. In 1971 the Crown Court was established and a red casting hood was introduced for criminal cases. Casting hoods are worn on the left side whereas High Court Judges wear the casting hood on the right shoulder.

Ede and Ravenscroft formerly issued all judges on appointment with a Judges' Robing List, last printed in 1933, containing details of dress to be worn. Much of this information can now be found in the Clerks'

KING'S BENCH DIVISION.

MICHAELMAS SITTINGS *Nisi Prius*	The Lord Chancellor's Breakfast and in Court on the First Day :—Court Coat, Waistcoat, and Knee Breeches of Black Cloth, Black Silk Stockings, Shoes and Steel Buckles, Scarlet Cloth Robe, Hood and Mantle trimmed with Ermine; Scarf, Girdle, Tippet, Plain Bands, Full-bottomed Wig, White Gloves and Beaver Hat. After First Day the same as Hilary Sittings.
HILARY SITTINGS *Nisi Prius*	Black Cloth Robe trimmed with Ermine; Girdle, Scarf, Tippet, Plain Bands and Tye Wig.
EASTER SITTINGS and TRINITY SITTINGS *Nisi Prius*	Purple Cloth Robe trimmed with Silk; Girdle, Scarf, Tippet, Plain Bands and Tye Wig.
SITTINGS IN BANCO	Same as above with the Hood in addition.
COURT OF CRIMINAL APPEAL	Scarlet Cloth Robe and Hood, Girdle, Tippet, Scarf, Plain Bands and Tye Wig. At Michaelmas and Hilary Sittings the Robe trimmed with Ermine. At Easter and Trinity Sittings the Robe trimmed with Silk.
MEETING OF JUDGES AT THE OLD BAILEY	Same as on First Day of Michaelmas Sittings.
ELECTION PETITIONS	Same as at *Nisi Prius*.
OLD BAILEY SESSIONS	Scarlet Cloth Robe, Girdle, Scarf, Tippet, Plain Bands, Tye Wig and Black Cap. At Michaelmas and Hilary Sittings the Robe trimmed with Ermine. At Easter and Trinity Sittings the Robe trimmed with Silk.
RED LETTER DAYS.	*Nisi Prius* :—Scarlet Robe, Girdle, Scarf, Tippet, Plain Bands and Tye Wig. When Sitting in Banco, Hood in addition. The Scarlet Robe and Hood worn during Michaelmas and Hilary Sittings are trimmed with Ermine. During Easter and Trinity Sittings the Scarlet Robe and Hood are trimmed with Silk. Jan. 25.—Conversion of Saint Paul. Feb. 2.—Purification of the B.V.M. „ 24.—Saint Matthias. Ash Wednesday (Movable). Mar. 25.—Annunciation of the B.V.M. Apr. 25.—Saint Mark. May 1.—Saint Philip and Saint James. „ 6.—His Majesty's Accession. Ascension Day (Movable). „ 26.—Birthday of H.M. The Queen. June 3.—Birthday of H.M. The King. „ 11.—Saint Barnabas. „ 22.—Coronation Day. June 23.—Birthday of H.R.H. the Prince of Wales. „ 24.—Saint John the Baptist. Celebration of H.M. The King's Birthday (Movable). „ 29.—Saint Peter. July 25.—Saint James. Oct. 18.—Saint Luke. „ 28.—Saint Simon and Saint Jude. Nov. 1.—All Saints'. „ 9.—Lord Mayor's Day. „ 30.—Saint Andrew. Dec. 21.—Saint Thomas.
CIRCUIT ROBES	To open Commission :—Scarlet Robe and Hood, Girdle, Scarf, Tippet, Plain Bands, Full-bottomed Wig and Beaver Hat. The same to Church. If Cathedral or University the Mantle and White Gloves in addition. Afterwards, change to Tye Wig, Robes, as at Old Bailey Sessions. *Nisi Prius* Robes the same as at London Sittings. When Dining with the Bishop, Court Coat, Waistcoat and Knee Breeches of Black Cloth, Black Silk Gown, Shoes and Steel Buckles, Tye Wig, Plain Bands and Silk Hat. Michaelmas and Hilary Sittings. Scarlet Robe trimmed with Ermine. Easter and Trinity. Scarlet Robe trimmed with Silk.

The second page of Ede and Ravenscroft's Judge's Robing List of 1933, formerly issued to all judges on appointment

Mrs Rose Batteson, an Ede and Ravenscroft robemaker, working on the Lord Chancellor's robe of black silk damask trimmed with gold lace and ornaments

Handbook, and dress worn by advocates in court is altered by Practice Directions. For instance, after members of the Institute of Legal Executives could become authorised advocates in 1998 the Lord Chancellor issued a practice direction stating that in the Supreme Court and Crown Courts Queen's Counsel wear a short wig and silk or stuff gown over a court coat, and junior Counsel wear a short wig and stuff gown with bands, and solicitors and other advocates wear a black stuff gown and bands but no wig. The Consolidated Criminal Practice Directions released in July 2002 state that in Magistrates' Courts advocates appear without robes or wigs.

In the words of Professor J. H. Baker, continuity or at least the appearance of continuity is a valuable asset to any legal system and people have more faith in a system that has stood the test of time. When serjeants-at-law had their robes put on them at an investiture ceremony dating back to the fourteenth century the Lord Chief Justice made a speech explaining the importance of a distinctive legal costume. A number of these speeches survive and are equally relevant to the wearing of robes by the Judiciary and Bar today. Among the reasons given for wearing robes were: 1) they reminded the wearer that he belonged to a disciplined profession with high standards of behaviour; 2) they indicated to the public at a glance who was an advocate; 3) they denoted rank within the profession, being the formal habit of a superior degree in law, and 4) they promoted gravity of bearing and good manners. Robes worn by English judges have continued unaltered in essentials for over six hundred years. In the twenty-first century it is of utmost importance to preserve the distinctive robes of our Bench and Bar as a symbol of the independence this country used to enjoy and of the continuity of the world's principal legal system.

Notes

'Can Thus Large Wigs our Reverence Engage?'

Page 9. 'Henry III . . . premature baldness': John Woodforde, *The Strange Story of False Hair*, p.14

9. 'thinning grey hair': Paul Johnson, *Elizabeth I: A Study in Power and Intellect*, pp.13–14

11. 'Roundheads . . . cut of their hair': F.W. Fairholt, *Costume in England: A History of Dress*, vol.1, pp. 307-9

11. 'Cromwell . . . as long as it would grow': Fairholt, 1, pp. 326–8

12. 'colour favoured by the King': Samuel Pepys, *Diary*, 2 November 1663

13. 'more Periwig than Man': reproduced in Fairholt, 1, p. 346

13. 'Sorts of Perawicks': Randle Holme, *Academy of Armory, or Storehouse of Armory and Blazon* , Book 2, chapter 18, 463

13. 'Women usually wear . . .': Holme, Book 2, chapter 17, 389

15. 'Full-bottom reached . . .': Woodforde, p. 28

15. 'a very odd Figure': Addison, *The Spectator*, no.129, 28 July 1711

16. 'beneath his Quality and Estate': Budgell, *The Spectator*, no.150, 22 August 1711

16. Portrait of Budgell in wig reproduced as the frontispiece to Volume III of Bond's edition of *The Spectator*, 1965

17. 'later known as the Rose-Bag': J. Stevens Cox, *An Illustrated Dictionary of Hairdressing and Wigmaking*, p. 132

18. 'as white as a miller's': Fairholt, 1, p. 346

19. 'nightcap wigs': Steele, *The Tatler*, no.30, 18 June 1709

20. 'Dorinda's letter': Budgell, *The Spectator*, no.319, 6 March 1712

21. 'Sciences of *Poetry* and *Dress*': Gay, *The Guardian*, no.149, 1 September 1713

21. 'Thomas Baker's comedy': Fairholt, 1, p. 347

22. '*The Triple Plea* ... early assault': David Bindman, *Hogarth and his Times*, plate 59

25. 'The Caxon': Cox, pp. 38–9

25. 'eighteenth-century dress code': Cox, p. 29

26. 'a style of Short Bob': Cox, p. 136

26. 'Odd Advertisements': *Annual Register,* 1759, p.169

29. 'Uncle Toby prepares to go courting': Laurence Sterne, *Tristram Shandy*, vol. 9, chapter 2

29. 'ashamed to be illiterate': James Boswell, *Life of Johnson*, 9 April 1778

32. 'The prevailing fashion . . .': Richard Fenton, *Memoirs of an Old Wig*, xv

32. Friedrich Klopstock: Coleridge, Samuel Taylor, letter, September 1798: Richard Holmes, *Coleridge: Early Visions* (1989), p. 208

34. 'every decent physician wore a wig': Maria Edgeworth, *Patronage*, chapter 20
34. 'General Whitford . . . name of White Wig': Fenton, xiv
34. 'length of regimental queues': Cox, p. 128
34. 'An illustration of *Camp Scenes*': Bryan Fosten, *Wellington's Infantry* (1), p.7
34. 'pleased to dispense with the use of queues': Thomas Carter, *Curiosities of War and Military Studies*, p. 184
35. 'hove overboard, with three cheers': Carter, p. 185
35. 'the last of the powderers': Michael Barthop, *Wellington's Generals*, p. 32
35. 'Wigs were worn by Bishops': Cox, p. 29
37. 'thought them so "coxcombical"': James Derriman, *Pageantry of the Law,* p. 37
37. 'How cold and dead a Figure': *The Spectator*, no. 407, 17 June 1712
39. 'a certain Mr Reverend Jessamy': *The Connoisseur*, no. 45, 24 April 1755 (390)
39. 'the shorter styles of Cut': Cox, p. 52
39. 'rather fuller than at present': Derriman, p. 37
40. 'ought to be asham'd': Richard Brinsley Sheridan, *St Patrick's Day*, II, iv
40. Humphrey Ravenscroft's patent: quoted in Una Campbell, *Robes of the Realm*, p. 27
41. 'refused to recognise son': Croake James, *Curiosities of Law and Lawyers*, p. 593
41. 'continued to grease': Derriman, p. 38
41. 'manufacture barristers' wigs': Campbell, p. 29
42. 'women barristers . . .the wig': Derriman, p. 38
42. 'medieval Order of the Coif': J. H. Baker, *The Order of Serjeants-at-Law*, pp. 69–73
42. 'Monumental effigies and brasses': W.T.N. Hargreaves-Mawdsley, *A History of Legal Dress in Europe,* pp. 54–5
42. 'wearing their velvet Coifs': pp. 486–8
43. 'wear their own hair': Hargreaves-Mawdsley, p. 66
43. 'portraits of serjeants': Baker (1984), plates IX–X
43. 'church of Mottram-in-Longdendale': Baker (1984) plate XII,1
45. *Paul before Felix* (Hogarth): Bindman, 1997, plate VI
45. 'this, a devil. . .': Ireland and Nichols, *Hogarth's Works*, vol.2, pp. 73–6
45. 'portrait of Sir Charles Abbot': Derriman, opp. p.161
46. 'satirical print . . . bald judge': Woodforde, 98
46. 'Judicial Costume': *The Leisure Hour* 26, pp.707-9
46. 'Ravenscroft's "new and improved design"': Campbell, p. 28

From Noble Robe to Ignominious Habit

51. 'plain, sleeved ankle-length surcoat': Hargreaves-Mawdsley, p. 88
51. '*De Laudibus Legum Angliae*': Derriman, p. 36
51. 'fifteenth-century monumental brasses': Baker, 1975, p.20, n.12
53. 'pleated tunica . . . a large purse or bag': reproduced in Baker, 1975, p.15
53. Whaddon Hall illuminations: three of them are

reproduced as the frontispiece and plates 11 and 12 in Hargreaves-Mawdsley

54. The brass at Hempstead of William Mordaunt: reproduced in Baker, 1975, p.16
54. The will of Robert Pynkney: P.C.C. Prob: 11 16/1
54. Thomas Jubbes: P.C.C. Prob: 11 25/7
55. 'not yet a prescribed uniform . . . sobriety of clothing': J. H. Baker, 'A History of the Gowns Worn at the English Bar', 1975
55. 'none . . . any light colours': Fairholt, p. 331
55. 'in tymes past . . . from the barr for your folish pride': Baker, 1975, p. 16
55. 'required to wear gowns . . . of the Inns of Court': Hargreaves-Mawdsley, p. 89
55. 'The monumental brass . . . of Thomas Palmer': reproduced in Baker, 1975, pp. 16–17
56. 'adorn'd with a Noble Robe': Sir Henry Chauncy, *Historical Antiquities of Hertfordshire*, p. 526
58. 'resume the wearing of . . . Bar-Gowns': Baker, 1975, p.18
58. 'One of these appendages': Derriman, pp, 34–5
58. 'cloven tongue': M.T. Riley, *Notes and Queries,* 1st series, vol. 9, (1854), p. 323
58. 'the wattles of a cock or turkey': J. S. Udal, *Notes and Queries*, 7th series (1887), 78
58. 'is not easy to describe in words', 'nor easy to draw clearly': Baker, 1975, pp.15, 20 ; Hargreaves-Mawdsley, p.118, fig. 8.
59. 'a wallet to carry his breviates in': Gentleman's Magazine; 1795,Vol.2, 562
59. 'without ruffling the sensibilities': J. S. Udal, *Notes and Queries,* 7th series (1887), 4,78
59. 'the verve with which he pleaded his case': Derriman, p.35
59. *Troilus and Cressida*, ed. Kenneth Palmer (1982), 212, III, iii, p.145n
61. 'derived from the medieval fashion of the *chaperon*': Hargreaves-Mawdsley, pp. 90, 119; *see also* E. McC., *Notes and Queries*, 7th series [1887], 4, 155
61. 'the *chaperon* became a distinctive feature of French advocates': Hargreaves-Mawdsley, p.36
61. 'so yow by this tabard': Baker, 1984, p. 288
63. an early sixteenth-century document: British Museum MS Harl. 6064, f.101
64. 'Many nineteenth-century contributors': *Notes and Queries*, 1st series vol.10,38, 213; vol.11,114; 7th series, vol.4,155
64. 'Why the *left* shoulder': Baker, 1975, p.19
64. 'on the left side only': Baker, 1984, p.487

Gown, Hood and Mantle: The Judge's Habit

65. Sir John Fortescue: Baker, 1984
66. 'when judges gave up wearing the collobium': the authority on most aspects of legal dress is Professor J. H. Baker and the best account of judges' robes is his 'A History of English Judges' Robes' in *Costume* (the journal of the Costume Society), no. 12 (1978), pp. 27–39

Sources and Bibliography

Anonymous, 'Judicial Costume', *The Leisure Hour* 26 (1877), pp. 707–9

Baker, J. H., 'A History of the Gowns Worn at the English Bar', *Costume* no. 9 (1975), pp. 15–21

—— 'A History of English Judges' Robes', *Costume*, no. 12 (1978), pp. 27–39

—— *The Order of Serjeants-at-Law*, Selden Society (1984)

—— 'An Outline History of the Legal Robes Now Worn in England and Wales', *Court Dress: A Consultation Paper issued on behalf of the Lord Chancellor and the Lord Chief Justice* (1992)

Barthop, Michael, *Wellington's Generals* (Osprey Men-at-Arms series, London, 1978)

Bindman, David, *Hogarth and his Times: Serious Comedy* (London, 1997)

——, *Hogarth* (London, 1981)

Boswell, James, *The Life of Samuel Johnson* (1791), ed. R.W. Chapman (Oxford, 1970)

Campbell, Una, *Robes of the Realm: 300 Years of Ceremonial Dress* (London, 1989)

Carter, Thomas, *Curiosities of War and Military Studies* (London, 1860)

Chauncy, Sir Henry, *Historical Antiquities of Hertfordshire* (1700)

Connoisseur, The, by 'Mr Town' (George Colman the elder and Bonnell Thornton), 2 vols (1755)

Cox, J. Stevens, *An Illustrated Dictionary of Hairdressing and Wigmaking* (rev. ed., London, 1984)

Cunnington, P. and Lucas, C., *Costumes for Births, Marriages and Deaths* (London, 1992)

Derriman, James, *Pageantry of the Law* (London, 1955)

Edgeworth, Maria, *Patronage* (1814)

Fairholt, F. W., *Costume in England: A History of Dress*, rev. ed. H. A. Dillon, 2 vols (1885)

Farquhar, George, *The Recruiting Officer* (1706), ed. Peter Dixon (Manchester, 1986)

Fenton, Richard, *Memoirs of an Old Wig* (1815)

Fosten, Bryan, *Wellington's Infantry* (1), (Osprey Men-at-Arms series, London, 1981) *Guardian, The* (March–October 1713), no. 149 (1713)

Hargreaves-Mawdsley, W. N., *A History of Legal Dress in Europe Until the End of the Eighteenth Century* (Oxford, 1963)

Holme, Randle, *The Academy of Armory, or Storehouse of Armory and Blazon Containing the several variety of Created Beings, and how born with Coats of Arms, both Foreign and Domestick. With the Instruments used in all Trades and Sciences, together with their Terms of Art* (Chester, 1688)

Ireland, John and John Nichols, *Hogarth's Works: With Life and Anecdotal Descriptions of his Pictures*, 3 vols (1883)

James, Croake, *Curiosities of Law and Lawyers* (1891)

Johnson, Paul, *Elizabeth I: A Study in Power and Intellect* (London, 1988)

Pepys, Samuel, *Diary*, ed. John Warrington, 3 vols (1906)

Scott, Sir Walter, *The Antiquary* (1816)

Shakespeare, William, *Hamlet* (1599–1601)

——, *Troilus and Cressida* (1602)

Sheridan, Richard Brinsley, *The Plays and Poems of Sheridan*, ed. R. C. Rhodes (Oxford, 1928)

Smart, Christopher, *Poetical Works: Miscellaneous Poems*, ed. Karina Williamson (Oxford, 1987)

Spectator, The (March 1711–December 1712, 1714), ed. Donald F. Bond, 5 vols (Oxford, 1965)

Sterne, Laurence, *The Life and Opinions of Tristram Shandy* (1759–67)

Tatler, The (April 1709–January 1711), no. 30, 18 June 1709

Warton, Thomas the Younger, *The Poetical Works*, (Oxford, 1802)

Wilson, Robert, *The Cobbler's Prophecy* (1594)

Woodforde, John, *The Strange Story of False Hair* (London, 1971)

Woty, William, *The Shrubs of Parnassus, Consisting of a Variety of Poetical Essays, Moral and Comic*, 'by J. Copywell of Lincolns Inn' (1760)

INDEX

Page numbers in italic refer to illustrations